The POWER of Collaboration

A New Vision for Victory

Foreword by Dr. George Fraser

Afterword By Dr. Ruben West

Submissions by the Following Authors:

Chis'mere Mallard

Johnny "MACKnificent" Mack

Edward C. Williams

Daryl Fletcher

Terrance "The Unstoppable Coach" Leftridge

Pastor Jonathan Haywood

Dr. Edward Womack

John McClung Jr

Collaboration

Definitions (3)

1.General: Cooperative arrangement in which two or more parties (which may or may not have any previous relationship) work jointly towards a common goal.
2.Knowledge management (KM): Effective method of transferring 'know how' among individuals, therefore critical to creating and sustaining a competitive advantage. Collaboration is a key tenet of KM.
3.Negotiations: Conflict resolution strategy that uses both assertiveness and cooperation to seek solutions advantageous to all parties. It succeeds usually where the participants' goals are compatible, and the interaction among them is important in attaining those goals.

Read more:
http://www.businessdictionary.com/definition/collaboration.html#ixzz44rg6KKcr

Foreword to Power of Collaboration
By Dr. George Fraser

It is not every day that I get to collaborate with likeminded individuals that are focused on working together for a celebratory cause, not competing against each other for position or prominence. So it was with a happy heart and speculative spirit that I agreed to work with the Men of Vision and write the foreword to this awesome and highly anticipated book. This eclectic group of young men have created a concept that is resonating with people far and wide.

"What if we came together in concert to support, encourage and promote each other. What could that type of Collaboration create"?

Well to date it has created five Best Selling books and made Amazon Best Selling authors of each of them. In addition their dreams of international speaking, coaching and entrepreneurship have been realized.

It is my distinct pleasure to share with the world a group of visionaries and entrepreneurs that have as their mission to Empower, Encourage, Enlighten and Educate men and women across the spectrum. This book is a result of that Collaboration., It witnesses the possibilities and potentialities of men and women when competition is removed from the equation.

I have spent My entire life sharing with others the gift of Networking for a common cause and a profitable platform of possibility. I am witnessing my teaching and systems come into fruition with the culmination of this book and the work of this Movement .

This is a model of how to network toward a common goal and purpose. The Power of Collaboration is in a nutshell, my life's work personified. Your cooperation is good but collaboration is better. Why? With cooperation one plus one equals two. With collaboration one plus one equals eleven. Collaborative efforts increase results exponentially. In this book you will find stories of hope and anticipation, you will finds words of wisdom and a new work ethic that suggests that together we not only can accomplish more, we can accomplish GREATNESS.

I had the pleasure of being a guest on Dr. Edward Womack's show recently and it not only showcased my dream and program, but also gave me insight into why the Men of Vision are becoming a force to be reckoned with from coast to coast.

Their model is devoid of the stereotypical snags and traps that pull others down. Instead they are advancing a reality that says "Let me help you reach your goals and in the process mine will come into view." For over forty years I've said to all that would listen "the best way to get what you want, is to find a way to give it"

It is the association with others that leverages each of us to loftier heights. The principles of *Power*Networking that I have so often espoused are evident in this concept and throughout this book. This Anthology features the Men of Vision and five other forward thinking entrepreneurs that "Get It" and they want to share it with you.

As you read each section, you get the rare chance to share a slice of their soul. They will allure you and assure you that working with each other rather than against each other is a smart and profitable thing to do. As is evidenced by each of these authors, you are not an island and cannot achieve long term sustainable success alone.

I admonish you to ingest the wisdom of this book and find you a team of collaborative individuals that you can mastermind with and in turn leverage yourself to the level you deserve and dream of. Indeed Collaboration is the formula along with proper *Power*Networking that can and will segment you and Position you to be able to catapult to your next level of life and success.

It is with honor and a happy heart that I endorse and encourage you to read, study and appropriate this book. It very well may be the Prescription for Success you have been yearning for. I know that as I was privileged to peruse it I left enlightened, empowered, encouraged and educated. I pray it does the same for you.

Respectively

Dr. George Fraser

Contact info for Dr. George Fraser

Dr. George C. Fraser is an international bestselling author and the founder of The *Power*Networking Conference (Forbes Magazine called it one of the top five Conferences to attend in the US. Period) His inaugural book "Success Runs in our Race", established him as a prolific transformational thought leader that is touching the lives of African American Entrepreneurs across the country.

He is unapologetic about swinging open doors of opportunity to those that have been long denied access. The annual Power Networking Conference has become the must attend conference in the African American community for the last 10 years.

In 2016 it was moved from Dallas Texas to being held in Prince Georges County Maryland. Dr. Fraser is a sought after Speaker and power broker that can speed dial all of today's top leaders. His Passion is to Empower and Enrich his audience. He can be reached at ..

gfraser@frasernet.com

Introduction:

The Power of Collaboration

Few things in life impact us more than interacting with others. In the process of that interaction many things transpire. Most notably of which is an inert and incessant need for Competition. Competition creates a crab mentality that tries to hold others down to prevent them from besting you. Our book The Power of Collaboration explores this myth and offers alternatives to this divisive practice.

These eight authors offer insight as to how collaboration is a tool to create Mutually Assured Success. Collaboration is a concept that says "When we work together, we are able to accomplish our own desires and assist you in reaching Theirs.

This school of thought negates the need for sabotage or subterfuge. It eliminates the negative behavior of competing with others and instead works with others to find a common good.

Each entry searches the subject of Cooperation and Collaboration and seeks to find a way to work with others instead of against them. This Collaboration can take place in entrepreneurial endeavors as well as community improvement concerns. Rather than trying to be the first or best or better than the others, this model suggests that we can and should work in one accord to reach greater heights and better results.

It is with that distinction that the authors of this book have submitted chapters relevant to that topic and instrumental towards paving a way to accomplish that goal without causing loss or lack to any intended party. Rather this is a method and manner that can and should leverage the playing field so that everybody wins, but not at the expense of any one.

Self Published Authors Network
P.O. Box 2111
Desoto Texas 75123
Tel: 214-469-747-3095
Ordering information
Quantity Sales. Special discounts are available in quantity purchases by corporations, associations, networking groups. For details contact info@MenOfVisionMovement.org at the address above

> **Individual Sales.** Self Published Authors Network publications are available online at and info@MenOfVisionMovement.org as both a paperback and an eBook.

The Power of Collaboration

Collaboration 2

Foreword to Power of Collaboration 3

   By Dr. George Fraser 3

Introduction 9

Chapter 1: My Journey to the Power of Collaboration 14

Chapter 2: To Dominate, You Need to Collaborate 40

Chapter 3: Association Brings about Collaboration 92

Chapter 4: Collaboration Makes your Why Work 102

Chapter 5: Collaboration: Why is the new What 118

Chapter 6: Be UNSTOPPABLE with Collaboration 126

Chapter 7: Collaboration from a Pastor's Perspective 140

Chapter 8: A Collaborative B.A.L.L (Born Again Lord Led) 158

Afterword 180

   By Dr. Ruben West 180

Chapter 1: My Journey to the Power of Collaboration

By: Dr. Edward Womack

The Beginning

Has anyone ever asked you "What is the most important thing you have learned in your lifetime?" Think about it. I'll bet you have an answer. Perhaps you would say something about implementing the Golden Rule, respecting the world, or how important it is to love one another. I'll bet though that your answer has to do with what you learned from your mistakes. You paid for your wisdom with errors. I have made many mistakes in my lifetime and learned some very valuable lessons. This book is the result of one of those experiences. You can't succeed alone. There is Power in Collaboration.

Working jointly with others in an intellectual endeavor is the most satisfying and successful stage of my life I have ever experienced. Our team, the Men of Vision, share expertise and our individual crafts to blend the noumenon of our creative powers into an original product that reaches a wider audience because of its depth and comprehensive coverage like the power of a woven cord.

The Power of Collaboration works because of the strength of the cord and the value of its individual threads. Each member of our team contributes unique gifts and experience. This book details how this process can benefit you and the dream you are building right now.

Perhaps if I start at the beginning you can relate more closely to the process that has evolved to generate our success and how the model can help you reach your own goals. I'd like to briefly cover the mistakes of my own life. I'm sure you have a few as well. Along with the low points, I also built a professional career, and like my peers on the team, I profited from learning what didn't work to build a plan that does!

The total process basically has a beginning, middle, and an end. If the beginning is a culmination of my life experiences, the middle is the production of my book Back From Broken and the formation of my dreams for the future, and the end, which of course is ongoing, is the combined efforts of our team and The Power of Collaboration.

My cycle on this journey we call life began in Detroit. The auto industry was booming and I was raised at a time when the "Motor City" was in the midst of its greatness. I'm sure the business impacted my drive for success. We lived in a middle class neighborhood. My mother was a nurse and my father was a police executive.

Unfortunately, the drug trade was also thriving in the area and temptations were high. I took my first sip of alcohol at ripe-old age of eleven. I experienced some pretty ugly situations in my neighborhood and my family, things that impacted my self-concept and security. Being violated physically disrupted the desire in me to fight back. I turned more to alcohol and drugs than I did relationships. I chose not to talk about the abuse for fear of rejection, especially from my father whom I respected. In spite of my difficult times, I learned a lot from my parents. I dedicated my book to my dad. He was the primary motivator that led me toward excellence in all of my positive pursuits.

I made many poor choices as I grew up. I allowed the stigmas, stereotypes, and unspoken codes mold my thinking and the resulting decisions. I grew up in an environment and time where men were not supposed to cry. Men do not show any weaknesses. As a child, I recall being told to keep my chin up and my mouth shut.

The abuse stopped long before high school and I became co-captain of my high school basketball team. I learned so much from that role of leadership and the value of teamwork. From basketball, I learned to love the freedom that comes from winning and the value of getting good grades in school. I started noticing how I was living and what I could do to be great. The reality was I was not living the life that I wanted to live.

After high school, I got a job at a local fast food spot that lasted a grand total of three weeks. I was raised in a predominately loving home with both of my parents present. I had gained numerous academic achievements and achieved athletic prowess. I attempted to go to a local college, but the haunting remnants of abuse continued to plague me and undermine my success. The process of running and hiding began. Honestly, I did not really know what was going on with me and I did not talk to anyone about it, so no one else understood me either.

I tried a coaching job, but I had trouble obeying the rules, so in 1985 I visited a USMC recruiter and entered a Military Entrance Processing Station at the State University in Detroit. I entered the Marine Corps and graduated from boot camp with the rank of E-3 Lance Corporal. I was so proud of myself. After Okinawa, the Philippines, and Korea, I returned to the States and met Juanita, the most beautiful woman I had ever seen in my life.

It's hard to encapsulate one's life into such a brief story, but somehow the marriage wasn't right. You ever hear of codependency. It means that humans by nature attach themselves to other people, other things, money, work, food, sex. It is natural, but that does not make it right. I think I had a codependency problem. When you put all your value in another person or thing, you lose your sense of identity or worth. You walk around feeling empty because your only success has been to please someone else. Codependents worry more about what is missing or things they cannot change. You focus more on the problem than the solution. Nothing was ever enough for me.

There were always peaks and valleys. I began to think something had to change and the marriage lost its value in my heart. In spite of the family, our children, my success, and my values, I was lost and lonely. If you have read my book, Back From Broken, this is where I talk about feeling broken.

I did not want to be married and I tried to transfer my unhappiness on others. As I said earlier, the most important lessons we learn from life come from our mistakes. I tried to live life alone, be self-sufficient, and shoulder the unhappiness that life included. The whole situation grew toxic and poisoned me in a way that was frightening and overwhelming.

Drugs, alcohol, arrests, poor choices. Those were the facets of my life. I was dishonorably discharged from the Marine Corps in 1991. Upon my General Court Martial and subsequent sentencing to two years in the brig, my wife left me. I merely existed now. I drank for days at a time. I became a crack addict. I was stuck in a crack cocaine, alcohol and weed induced cloud of escape. I had no idea where I was supposed to go or what path I should take.

At this point, it would have helped if I had looked in the mirror like the exercise I recommend in my book. If you feel any doubt about your future, I suggest this process to evaluate yourself. Somehow, I lost everything I ever hoped for. It was gone. Everywhere I turned, there was a wall.

What a complicated knot. I felt like it was too late to change, too hard. I will never be the man I was. Did you ever experience that? Then you know what it is like to hit rock-bottom.

The Transition

I was broken. I know what it is to fight loss, addiction, and pain. Like it says in God's Word, "I know what it is to be in need, and I know what it is to have plenty" (Phil. 4:12). I've been rich; I've been poor. I thought success was how much money I made, how cool I looked, and how many people worked for me. Something happened though that helped me to learn the secret of being content.

I did not understand Paul's words: "I have learned the secret of being content in any and every situation, whether well fed or hungry, whether living in plenty or in want. I can do everything through him who gives me strength" (Philippians 4:12-13). My life was one big knot. If you have been there, you know you cannot do it alone. You need help.

I was exhausted and lost, overwhelmed with the feeling of emptiness and hopelessness. I had chosen to give up rather than reach out. Remember I said this was the lesson I had to learn to build The Power of Collaboration. Do you know your time of turning that brought you back from broken, back to freedom? Did you make a choice?

The choice I made was inside my soul. I lived in darkness from an addiction to crack. The road to self-destruction turned to a path of despair, void of all hope. Now I just wanted to die slowly and watch my problems fade into death. Sitting on a concrete bench in Decatur, Georgia, I watched a line of ants swarm around a piece of bread near my feet. I saw no purpose, no value in their pitiful size or duty. The thought of crushing those ants seemed empowering. I wished someone would put me out of my misery too.

It occurred to me though how productive they were, lifting fifty times their body weight to provide for their community. They were not afraid of me or anything that got in their way. Those little ants were ready to die. What a contrast to me. I had not showered in two weeks and I had been hooked on crack for eighteen months. What a waste of human flesh.

I felt the sun blazing on my face as if until that moment I had ignored its existence (and God). I wanted to pretend the last thirty years of my life had never happened. I wanted   the nightmare to be over. Somehow watching those ants move a piece of bread a thousand times their weight inspired me to change. I walked away from that bench and got help.

The days characterized by gluttony, lying, cheating, drug use, deceiving others and myself died that day. From that day forward, I focused on dreams, aspirations, and potential. I turned to God. I asked for help.

Over time, I learned to listen to God for a plan. Today I have come to know and trust Christ as my Savior. He not only saved me from an internal hell on earth, which I had created for myself, but the hell of the streets where I thought I could find refuge. I am more blessed now than what I thought I was when I was making all that money and conforming to the rules of society.

The Middle

The middle of the process for me was the decision to serve others. The first thing I had to do was look in the mirror and see what I had to work with. Not only did I "need" to write a book, but also the book I wrote summarizes the entire process of growth I had to endure to get where I am today. I hope you get the chance to read Back from Broken as it builds on everything I have summarized so far in this chapter. Once you read the book, you will understand more about my story. I would paraphrase my expertise as an urban leadership strategist.

I have 20+ years of experience as an IT professional. My recovery experience includes depression, substance abuse, and addiction with seven years sobriety. You can go to my website, www.manriseup.com, and view more of what I do individually. I have a radio show through the Survival Radio Network called Man Rise Up Radio (www.manriseupradio.com) that airs every Saturday at 11a.m EST.

The other thing I accomplished was to found the T.I.P.S. Academy, LLC an acronym for "Training Important People to Soar" TIPS is a service-oriented business with a mission to inspire, empower, encourage, and coach independent thinkers to effectively realize their destiny and fulfill their God-given purpose in life. This is accomplished by participating in community events, pertinent seminars, and training sessions designed to inspire, challenge, and equip participants with the confidence that there are no limits to what they are capable of accomplishing.

The Academy coaches male participants aged 13-28, the age group in greatest need of direction. I think what is important to note here are not the things I did, but that I had goals that I started on my own that thrived only through the "power of collaboration" which I will build on shortly.

I currently serve on the board of directors for the Trinity Community Ministries, the exact program that turned me around and put me on the path I am on now. My life had taken a turn for the better. I was progressing in the right direction. I had learned that it was okay to make mistakes if you learn from them. I learned that it is not how those problems affect you, but how you handle the adversity and grow from it. More than any time in my life, I did not want to quit. I knew I was not going to fail. I felt the energy growing inside me. I was ready for more so I reached out to find more cords to make a stronger rope in the goals that I believed in with all my heart.

Networking

How? I turned to social media and Facebook. Networking. The door to success opened. We are blessed to have everything we need to make connections on our phone, our laptops, our IPADS. So quick and convenient. I saw a cartoon once where everyone is standing around in heaven looking at his or her empty hands. I know we spend too much time on electronic devices now, but for this purpose, it is key in The Power of Collaboration. Networking is how I have benefitted and grown since Back From Broken. The success I experience daily is embracing the accelerated growth through collaboration.

One of the first prizes I won in my quest for collaboration was to meet an amazing coach named Dr. Ruben West. Over time I have learned so much from Dr. West, increased my confidence as a speaker, and shaped my own character as a confidence generator thanks to his guidance. Dr. West is the owner and founder of Black Belt Speakers.

Entering into a relationship has not only helped me to improve my transformational speaking, but also evolved into a mentorship, friendship and actual mobilization of ideas that would have taken a lot longer had I done it all alone. How does that happen? I handed control of my life over to God, so I believe in His guidance and intervention, but I also believe you have to have a plan and move forward with some direction like Dr. Fraser said in the Introduction: a plan, a power, and a prayer.

What we are doing here is significant, but I also understand you are reading this to accomplish your own goals. My recommendation at this point is that you have "looked in the mirror" (an exercise from my book Back From Broken), written down your goals, formulated at least a preliminary plan, and added prayer to the agenda. The power will come as you start to network and add contacts to the list you are building under that plan.

Dr. George Fraser, our keynote speaker and coach, endorsed this book and stands as a model of success for Men of Vision. Dr. Fraser is Chairman and CEO of FraserNet, a company he founded to lead a global networking movement that brings together diverse human resources to increase opportunities for people of African descent. Dr. Fraser understands what it is to live without as he grew up on the streets of New York with no expectations.

He is also a successful businessperson, leader, author, and humanitarian. He has a wealth of experience as a leader and coach and molds our efforts in many positive ways. Not unlike the Power of Collaboration, Dr. Fraser has focused on PowerNetworking and contributed in many ways to our cause.

There are five of us who collaborate under the mission title of Men of Vision and others who are heavily involved in our growth like Dr. Fraser and Dr. West. Terrance Leftridge is our unstoppable coach. He helped us to see you need to do more than have a dream and he showed us how to live our dreams. John Mcclung Jr. is the owner/founder of "I Am a Testimony Clothing" Line (testimonyIam.com), a man who put action into our ideas and made it happen. Johnny "MACKnificent" Mack is the owner/founder of SPAN (Self-Published Authors Network). Mr. Mack co-founded Men of Vision and coaches others pursuing their dreams. Edward C. Williams is a coach and the owner/founder of Power Life Empowerment.

Our team is a perfectly matched jigsaw puzzle of expertise and energy that fits together to generate unbelievable results that benefit all of us and others. That, my friends, is what the power of collaboration is all about.

Success

Within 13 months, our team had four Amazon Bestsellers. We hosted the Reclaim the Flame conference in 2015. Motivated in a single purpose to succeed and supported academically as a group, we moved into additional markets both separately and under our joint efforts as Men of Vision.

The Men of Vision Business Empowerment Tour we are building this year is guaranteed to provide others with the proven techniques, strategies, tools, and motivation to deliver the best system advice yet. Dr. Fraser and Dr. West continue to be involved and coach our efforts, an important inoculation to continued success. The Men of Vision created an Amazon bestseller called Reclaim the Flame last year, which was a book, created from excerpts of all five of our individual books.

Building the teamwork and combined energies and knowledge, we share as Men of Vision has afforded the true practice of collaboration vs. competition where the five founding members of individually owned private businesses were able to band together, egos aside, and lend individual and collective exchange, accountability, and creativity for the exposure. Bestselling book creations, major conferences, specialized publicity, letters directed to the right audience, endorsements, interchange of ideas, and delegation of duties...these are some of the pieces of our master puzzle that have linked each of us together in a blended and continually expanding mural of success.

What next? My colleagues and I will continue to host conferences and build on our tour. We sent out letters to entrepreneurs and Atlanta businesspersons to invite them to join us in a collaborative effort to produce a book of prestigious work from qualified sponsors knowing the significant impact it could have on the participants and future readers. George Fraser, our keynote speaker for the Powerlife Conference agreed to write the foreword to this anthology.

That is huge! Dr. Fraser is a world-renowned speaker, New York Times bestselling author and founder of one of the most important conferences offered every year. Dr. Ruben West, also a bestselling author and internationally recognized speaker has agreed to do the afterword.

You can find experts in your field through your own networking efforts. Attend conferences. Find the areas online where communication is happening in your field. Invite other experts to meet with you, to collaborate on a conference or a book. There is so much more power in the combined effort.

The product has more credibility and the public does not make the same assumptions they do considering individual authors or entrepreneurs. Ask each author to present a submission of 5-10 pages with a positive, powerful, and uplifting message. It should speak to your focus; ours was the African American experience, focusing on collaboration over competition.

The overarching theme is we can achieve much more when we work together as opposed to walking alone. Organize your website. Email submissions. The letter we sent out reminded the participants they are "highly recommended". You need to do the research in your field to reap these kinds of rewards.

It is important to have a management process. Your team needs to include all the expertise you need to produce the desired effect. Put someone in charge of every duty required. Set objectives, smart objectives. The objectives should be clearly understood rather than flowery unobtainable ideas. Stick to concrete steps to achieve desired results. Design a way to measure those objectives so everyone knows when you have obtained results.

That might be financial goals or involve some kind of numbers, as in selling books, or just checking off goals obtained. You lose credibility if you do not accomplish anything concrete. Be realistic about your objectives and the time you allow to achieve them. The objectives are a key part of your success as they direct the members of your team toward clear goals and measure each member's commitment to the success of achieving those objectives. Balance collaboration and focus.

Whatever processes you set up will be seen as a sign of your style. If you all follow the objectives, success is inevitable and trust builds throughout the group. If not, members distance themselves from the rest of the group. There needs to be a manager who properly motivates others with the ongoing process of networking and supervision without being "in charge".

That person has qualities that are fair, effective, wise on how much time is allowed for any given task, and effective because of expertise and character. If members of the group are unrealistic, greedy, bureaucratic, out of touch with reality, overly complex, contradictory, or incompatible with others, you need to rethink your team.

Someone in the group needs to foster creativity. Listen to their imagination. Make creativity a focal point of your company in a collaborative environment. Set up regular brainstorming sessions to involve everyone. Great companies all value the power of collaboration and understand how to foster it within a team.

Finally, continue to incorporate technology in your plan and process. Technology is the fuel of our engines today. Companies will invest thousands into advanced technology before hiring more staff, so creative thinkers are important, but technology joins you together like the roads and planes that unite us in any given city physically.

I believe "To whom much is given, much is required" and I have made it my life's work to uplift and educate male youth in need. In addition, I want to continue to learn all I can so I can better myself and help others to be better and more successful in life. This is where the value of collaboration is so essential. I am improving because of what my fellow leaders have taught me and it rolls over to the men we are working with. The education is so much more comprehensive than it would have been back when I was the only one generating clients for the T.I.P.S. Academy. Our Powerlife Business Empowerment Conference is one-step further toward helping others learn the power of collaboration and the role of empowerment in business.

Learning about branding and marketing were accelerated by entering into the relationship with Peak Performers Institute who aided in the creation of the Man Rise Up brand and provided a significant transition from TIPS Academy seamlessly. My peers were also pivotal in helping me to transition from my personal title of "Life Transformer" to "Urban Leadership Strategist." The acceleration was mainly seen in the rebranding and creation of graphic and written copy. If you ever need me to bring this story and message of hope to your meeting, seminar, classroom, or event, I am available for bookings through any of the above websites. There are many life-saving principles to offer that has helped lead thousands to the success and happiness we all deserve.

I generated everything I do alone, but it was not until I hooked up with these other associates that the ministry took off like a rocket launched toward infinity. I am living proof that the peaks and valleys of life can be overcome. With the right information, a commitment to self-awareness and a dedication to serve others, our team has proven men can come together and do something significant. Our program offers practical insights to help others maximize their individual potentials under the power of an organized team through the process of collaboration.

Since you have taken the time to read this, you obviously care about improving and building a team to see your dreams into reality. You're human, so you have made mistakes like the rest of us, but you have learned from the mistakes and you are ready to push yourself toward success and change the world.

You are doing things you have never done before and you can taste the changes in your life and envision the presents of success under the tree of triumph. Oscar Wilde said, "Experience is simply the name we give our mistakes," so know that as you continue to grow there will be more mistakes, but as you acquire more wisdom, there will be more success.

Do not waste energy trying to cover up the failures; move on to the next challenge. Lean on our team. We are here to help you climb the ladder as you excel. Helen Keller said, "Alone we can do so little, together we can do so much." Come aboard, men and women of vision. The Power of Collaboration is yours.

I would be remiss, If I did not leave you with this: "Good, better, best, we cant let it rest, until our Good is our better and our Better is our Best.

I promise you in closing if you embrace the Power of Collaboration, "We will see you at the Top, because the bottom is too crowded"

Contact Info for Dr. Edward Womack

Dr. Edward Womack is the Urban Leadership Strategist. He is a co-founder of The Men of Vision among many of his Major Accomplishments. Dr. Womack is an Amazon best Selling Author of two books and is the founder of Man Rise Up a unique platform that allows men to Identify and overcome barriers in their Social, financial, spiritual and Entrepreneurial Lives. Dr. Womack is an international speaker, coach and social media specialist. His thought provoking insight and unique laser focused coaching style is in demand nationwide as he shares proven techniques, tips and tidbits on Collaboration and connectivity. He can be reached at...

dred@manriseup.com

Check him out every Saturday morning on Man Rise Up radio on the Survival radio network

He is available for Coaching, Keynote Speaking, Conferences, Seminars, panels, webinars and presentations

Chapter 2: To Dominate, You Need to Collaborate

By: Chis 'mere Mallard

W e are all fascinated by the image of the lone wolf hero, who accomplishes great things. I don't care if you're talking about Rambo taking out a whole platoon of bad guys single-handed, a sports figure who makes the Hall of Fame or an entrepreneur who starts a business from scratch and builds it up to a billion dollar corporation, we want a hero. That's why we are fascinated by figures like Captain America, Iron Man and Rocky Balboa.

But the reality is, there are few lone-wolf heroes. Even those who seem like they are out there fighting on their own have a whole team of people standing behind them, holding them up. A fighter pilot seems to be a lone warrior, but if it wasn't for the team of about 20 mechanics, electronic technicians and armorers who work on his airplane, he couldn't get that plane off the ground. While the pilot gets all the glory, his team, from the plane captain down, deserves it just as much.

The military thrives on teamwork, at least as much as any sports team you can think of. Anyone who has spent any time in uniform understands that. Soldiers, sailors, airmen and Marines all spend countless hours in training; turning individuals into members of a team. It is only by working as a team, with each member doing their own part and having confidence in their team-mates to do theirs, that any military organization is able to accomplish their mission.

Ultimately, our nation's entire military is one big team, albeit broken down into many separate parts. Each part is able to function on its own, with the right support; but they are all able to come together in support of that infantry soldier who is out there holding the ground.

To put that in perspective, there are about 1.3 million people in the United States military, with another 811,000 in the reserves. Only about 40,000 of them are infantry. That means that for every infantry soldier out there holding that crucial piece of ground, there are 32.5 people supporting them in one way or another. That support could be anything from driving tanks to bringing supplies, providing medical services to providing information about the enemy, flying a bomber mission to shooting a cannon; but in one way or another, everyone else is ultimately in a support role to the infantry.

If Rambo needs 32.5 people to support him (and he probably actually needs a lot more than that), then what's to make any of us think that we can go it on our own? The truth is, that any time we try to do things on our own, we are setting ourselves up for failure. We need others to help us succeed. Those others are called a TEAM.

Yeah, I know, that's not a new word to you. We all know about teams and their importance. But even in knowing, we don't always do what we need to. There's too much of a tendency to try to do things on our own and be that lone wolf hero. But while that makes for a nice story, it doesn't make for success.

Henry Ford had a great understanding of the concept of teamwork. Before Ford Motor Company, cars were built one at a time, by highly experienced craftsmen. Each one was original, sometimes in minor ways and sometimes in major ones. But this process required highly skilled individuals, who worked thousands of hours to produce one car.

The assembly line tapped into the power of teamwork. Each individual on the line became a specialist in doing one single thing. They would do that over and over again, finding the most efficient way of doing it. Along the way, they became so good at doing that one thing, that they all but eliminated the problems with doing it. So, not only did Ford's company build cars faster and cheaper than anyone else, but they also built better quality ones. Maybe they weren't as fancy as some of the other offerings out there, but you could count on them to last.

Ford's true genius was in grasping the value of a team and applying it to a new arena. Before him, nobody had tried using such a big team to build something too complex. But since Ford introduced the concept of the assembly line, everyone else has jumped on board and copied him.

Of course, Ford's idea of teamwork required a huge team, due to the complexity of the product he was creating. So, his teamwork had to go far beyond the factory floor. He had to build a team that included everything from procurement through manufacturing to sales. Ultimately, he built the first truly modern manufacturing company, big enough to mass produce cars and bring the price down to the point where cars were no longer a novelty for the wealthy, but a convenience for the middle class.

Just like the entire military team supports the efforts of the infantry soldier in the field, Ford's manufacturing team supported the efforts of the salesman on the car lot. Instead of everyone working to help the infantry soldier hold that all-important piece of ground, everyone on the team worked to help that salesman make that all-important sale.

There were a number of amazing results of Ford's manufacturing team concept, many of which were truly revolutionary:

- The concept of the assembly line changed manufacturing forever.
- The number of labor hours to build a car dropped to the point where it changed the way cars were sold.

- Cars became consistent, making it easier for salesmen to know their product.

- The price of the Model T car dropped to the point of becoming affordable to the middle class.

- Standardization of parts made repairs easier and cheaper.

- Mechanics only had to learn one system, as the same system would be used in all cars made by the company.

- People could order spare parts and repair their own cars, without having to know how to build or modify those parts. Some people actually ordered a car in parts, as they could afford them, and assembled it themselves.

- Customers would know in advance exactly what they were ordering.

- Ford was able to raise the standard wages of his assembly workers to the point where his employees were able to become his customers as well.

Ultimately, the biggest thing that Ford's team did for him was to make Ford Motor Company a success. In a time when car manufacturers numbered in the hundreds, most of them being small shops hand-building a few cars at a time, Ford became the industry giant, which caused his company to survive, while most of those companies folded after a few short years.

There's something truly amazing that happens when people work together as a team. It's called "synergy." This oft-misunderstood word simply means that the effect on people or organizations working together is much greater than just the sum of the parts. The cars that Ford produced were greater than any number of people could build on their own and the company that he built ended up being far greater than the sum of each one working on their own.

Synergy multiplies the strengths of those working together, while minimizing their weaknesses. It's easy to understand if you think of two bulls yoked together, pulling a wagon. One bull might be able to pull 10,000 pounds and the other 9,000 pounds. But when they are yoked together, those two bulls can't only pull a mere 19,000 pounds, but rather something like 35,000 pounds. The synergy of working together has multiplied their ability.

While the synergy of those bulls pulling together has increased their combined strength, it has also reduced any weaknesses they had. What if one of those bulls was blind? If you harnessed it to the wagon by itself, it probably wouldn't move. But harnessed together with another bull that could see, the blind bull would count on the sighted one to see for both of them. It would work as if it could see.

Pretty much any time you have someone on a team with a weakness, you can count on there being someone else on that team who is strong in that area. The one who is strong in that area will take care of it, while the weaker member will concentrate on areas in which they are strong.

This is one of the truly beautiful things about a team who has learned how to work together. Each team member will come to know the strengths of each other. Then, when there is a need, it will be natural for the team member who is strongest in that area to fulfill that need. If there are several team members who can fulfill that need equally well, then the decision about who does it can be made based upon other needs that the team has.

In this way, a team that is used to working together can reach a point where it seems as if there are no weaknesses in the team. Granted, the weaknesses will still be there and there will still be other teams who are stronger; but even so, the weaknesses won't be noticed due to how smoothly the team accomplishes their goals.

Sadly, there are many people who try to win the game, without ever taking the time to build their team. This is about as foolish as going out on a football field and facing off against a trained opponent by yourself. You're not going to win. Maybe there are some sports you can win at without having a whole team out there on the field; but even then, you have coaches and other team members, behind the scenes, who help the athlete prepare and compete.

Gathering a team requires much more than just picking any available body. There are always people who will be a detriment to the team, rather than an asset. As a leader, you have to be able to recognize these problem people. You also have to be able to recognize those who will be an asset. In fact,

I'd say that picking and preparing your team is the single most important thing that you'll ever do.

This requires a change in your own thinking. Rather than thinking of what you can do alone, you have to start thinking in terms of what your team can do. If you can't see the difference between the two, then you don't have a vision for your team yet. You've got to be able to see what the team can do, that you can't do, as well as what you're going to have to do to make that team effective.

Let's get this straight; your job isn't to do everything yourself, it's to assemble a team that can accomplish the vision that you have. That means breaking down the vision into specific tasks, skills and requirements. Once you have that, then you can start thinking about what sort of people can accomplish each of those tasks and requirements. This goes much farther than just what sorts of skills they have, as often what sort of a person they are will make more of a difference than what sort of skills they have.

I've hired people before and I learned early on that the personality of the person makes more of a difference than their education. You can always find lots of people who are "qualified" by education and training for a job, but that doesn't mean that they have the right temperament for it. Can you imagine someone with a personality like Archie Bunker being part of your customer service team? They'd run off your customers, no matter how qualified they are.

The flip side of that coin is that people with the right temperament can always be taught the necessary skills. It's easy to teach someone skills, but it's next to impossible to change their temperament.

Sadly, in today's entitlement society, it's becoming harder and harder to find the right sort of people. All too many have the attitude that you owe them something, rather than having a good work ethic. You don't need people like that; you need people who will catch hold of your vision and treat it as their own. People like that don't need to be constantly supervised and motivated, because they motivate and supervise themselves.

So, when you're trying to pick out the kinds of people you need, don't just think of skills; think of their personalities. Think of people who you will be able to count on. Think of people you'll be able to trust. And don't forget to think about people who you will enjoy working with.

Vision

Once you find those people, then you need to infect them with your vision. You see, visions are one of those things that can't be taught, they have to be caught. So you have to become infectious. Oh, you can usually explain it to others in a matter of a few minutes, but that doesn't mean that they've got it. At best it means is that they understand it. There's a world of difference between the two and you need people who are as on-board with your vision as you are.

The only way a team can truly work as a team is if they are all on board, working towards the same goal. If even one team member is missing that goal, then it affects the whole team. It can affect it enough that the team never reaches the goal.

There are many different ways of managing a team, but much fewer ways to lead it. Leadership is much different than management in that it pulls people together to follow the leader towards a common goal, whereas management pushes people towards accomplishing it. The problem is, when you push people, they may end up going off in strange directions. It's about like tying to herd cats.

That's why you need to become infectious with your vision. Your vision is the goal and everyone on the team needs to catch it. Then, and only then, will you have a team of people who are pulling together, trying to reach the same place. Each individual will take ownership in your vision, causing them to become as committed to it as you are.

If you can get your people to that point, you've accomplished your biggest task. You see, once they are committed to the vision, they'll give it all they've got. That's when people start thinking about the project in their off hours. That's when new ideas flow. That's when they reach deep down inside themselves, to give the project everything they've got. Your team magically transforms itself from a simple group of ordinary workers, into a team of energized winners.

The truly great thing about this is that once you get to that point, it's like nothing can stop your team. You no longer have problems motivating people. Discipline problems melt away. So do fights, disagreements and petty rivalries. The only disagreements you'll be left with are ones about the best way to do something; and those arguments will even look different.

When people become truly committed to something, they make it happen, regardless of what it takes. They'll go that extra mile, make that extra push, find that extra ounce of energy and push through the things that are getting in the way. Just like a sports team that pushes through to victory, a business team that is committed to fulfilling a vision will push through and do whatever is necessary to achieve their victory.

Have you ever watched a professional football team during a game? To the untrained eye, it looks like total confusion. Some players are running one way, while others are running another way. The guys on the line are all grunting and pushing, to keep the other team from breaking through. At best, it looks like barely controlled mayhem. But in fact, it's as tightly choreographed as the ballet.

Each of those team members has a particular task to do. The linemen are there to protect the quarterback. His job is to get the ball to whoever is going to make the yardage for the team, whether by handing it off to a runner or throwing it to a receiver. The runners have to be experts in finding holes in the opponent's line to sneak through and the receivers have to be faster than their opponents, while being able to catch a football at full running speed.

Even in plays where runners carry the ball, the receivers have a job; to distract the other team. Likewise, runners do the same for the receivers when the ball is thrown. If the receivers don't do a convincing job of making it look like they are getting into position to catch the ball, then the runners have to face more opposition; likewise for the runners, when the ball is thrown.

But they are all working together to accomplish the same goal. That is, to get that ball 100 yards down the field, past the opposing team. That requires a combination of skills; but more than anything, it requires the whole team working together. Most of those plays are timed and choreographed to the point where if one player is one foot out of position or one second early, the whole thing falls apart.

How can the team work together so effectively? They all have the same vision. They're all willing to suborn their own goals, dreams and aspirations to that vision. That's really something, considering that some of those football players have really big egos to go with their really big paychecks.

The vision comes from the coach. He's the one who puts the plan for the game together and trains his team in how to execute it. During the game, he's there on the sideline, like a general marshalling his forces. From that position, he makes the decisions of who will play and what plays they will accomplish to move that ball down the field. But he doesn't play himself.

This is an important point. The coach isn't the one who plays the game, although he is probably the single most important person, with the greatest ability to ensure that the team wins.

His role is actually more important than that of the players, as it effects what each and every one of them do. More than that, he affects how the team works together. Without the coach to pull them together and give them commonality of purpose, it isn't a team out to win a victory, it's a mob of overgrown goons, fighting over a ball.

You see, being that lone ranger is like being the coach, trying to play the game all by yourself. I don't care how good you are, you're not going to be able to do the job of 11 highly trained specialists, who have spent their professional lives learning their jobs. It doesn't matter that you're the one that trained them or that you know how to do all of their jobs. There's no practical way that you can do them all.

If you've decided to go forward without creating a team to surround yourself with, then you've basically decided to lose. Winning takes a lot of preparation, effort and skill. There's no way you can make it on your own. Those who decide not to gather a team together and infect them with their vision, don't end up accomplishing anything. They spend their time spinning their wheels, trying to gain traction.

You can keep going like you are; spinning your wheels, doing things on your own, and you'll never get anywhere. Or, you can decide to build and train a team, and find yourself launched forward into victory. It's all up to you.

But, I Can't Afford a Team

I can hear it now. Somewhere out there are a bunch of people reading this who are saying to themselves, "He doesn't understand. I can't afford a team. I don't have the budget to create one." I've got to do it on my own... at least until I make enough to hire that team.

Let me take a moment to destroy that argument. First of all, you'll never make it enough on your own, so that you can afford to hire your team. Even thinking you can is a false hope. You would have to work long hours, for years, to get to the point that a team can get to in even one year. There just aren't enough hours in the day to do everything yourself, and you're not talented enough to be an expert in everything you need to do.

So, you need that team so that you can get to the point where you can afford the team. But that doesn't mean you need to   go out and hire a bunch of people, paying them money you don't have. You can try to get a business loan, so that you have that money. Yes, that's one way you can do it; but it's not the only way.

What if I were to tell you that you can create a team, without spending a single dollar? Well, maybe you'll have to buy a few cups of coffee and a couple of lunches; but that's about it. You can assemble a team, get everyone on board and start towards victory, without that huge investment in manpower.

You do that through the power of strategic partnerships. What are those? They are partnerships between your business and other businesses, where you work together towards a common goal. You can either pay them just for the work that they do, or you can arrange to pay them out of your profits. You can even work out an arrangement where they are doing their part on a percentage basis.

This is actually much more common than you might think. Many chain stores rent their space in the mall on a percentage basis, rather than a fixed sum. That gives the mall an opportunity to make more money in the long run, because during the Christmas shopping season, they get a larger check. But when the store is setting up, they don't have to pay a thing.

There are many other examples of such partnerships, because they have become a common way of doing business. Most startups can't afford to pay out a bunch of money off the bat, so they work out these partnerships. Then, as they grow, their team members do too.

One of the greatest modern examples of this is the chain of home improvement centers, The Home Depot. The founders opened their first store on a concept of teamwork, excellent customer service and a small loan. But from there the chain has grown into a giant in the home improvement niche.

Really, the opening of the first Home Depot store was about several teams. First, there was the store team, which consisted of experts in the products that they sold and their use. Unlike most other lumberyards and hardware stores, when you talk to an associate in Home Depot, they have used the products they are selling and can tell you how to.

The Power of Collaboration

The other big team was the store's suppliers. There was no way they could fully stock that first store with the money they had available. So, they worked together with their suppliers to give the illusion of being fully stocked. Warehouse shelves were stacked high with empty boxes, rather than inventory. But to those first customers, the store looked full. But here's the key; the suppliers were ready to move large quantities of inventory into the store, and did so, the night after their grand opening. What had been sold was replenished and more, for the next day's business.

It is exactly this sort of out of the box idea which marks many modern business success stories. The founders couldn't afford to do everything they needed, so they found a new way to create their team. They hired their employees, but built a team relationship with their suppliers.

Another way to build a team is to use freelancers. These are people who work on contract to complete certain tasks or projects for a company. Many companies are trending towards hiring these freelancers, through websites like Upwork.com and

Guru.com, who connect freelancers and potential clients together.

Using freelancers allows an entrepreneur to hire expertise that they need, without having to hire the person full-time. Nor are there any of the expenses of providing the freelancer with an office, a computer or a phone line. They work from home and provide those things themselves.

These freelancers can be just as dedicated and hard-working team members as employees, or even more so. The best of them bring years of experience to the table, experience that you would normally have to pay a fortune for, if you were to hire the person full-time. Their experience allows them to provide ideas and suggestions which can help your ideas go forward towards success.

You see, those freelancers want you to succeed. That's because their success is directly tied to yours. Unlike employees who get paid to sit there and do nothing; they only get paid for the work that they do. This often causes them to be much more dedicated workers, who get things done quickly and efficiently.

The key to getting the most out of any freelancer is making them feel like they are part of the team. Don't just hire a freelancer to do a job, bring them on board with the vision and goals of your company. The more they know, the more they will be able to contribute. If you only hire them for specific tasks, without getting them on board with your vision, you'll never allow them to reach the full potential of the help they can be to you.

Gathering Your Team

Any team is all about the people you choose. You've got to have the right people to make it work. So your biggest job as a leader is to pick the right people. People who will be an asset to your team and not become a problem for it; who will bring fresh ideas and energy to the table, not steal the energy that others bring; who can catch the vision, mix well and work together with others.

For a team to become more than the sum of its parts, each part has to mesh together with the others, just like the gears in a fine watch. If one tooth of one gear has a burr on it or is out of alignment, it can bring the whole watch to a stop. Likewise if one of your team members has a rough edge that rubs the rest of the team the wrong way.

This may very well end up in conflict with other requirements you have for team members. Your first pick for a particular member may not be the best, simply because they don't work well as part of a team. Just being the best at what they do isn't enough, if they aren't a team player.

Ultimately, what you're after is the best possible team, not the best individuals. Remember, you want to develop synergy in your team. That can't happen if you have a team full of prima-donnas and lone wolves. Those individuals may add to the team, but they won't be able to bring the multiplication that you want. Your team will merely be a sum of its parts, not the one that goes beyond that to becoming much more than that sum.

If you think about it, it would take a really incredible individual to make up for the loss of multiplied ability that synergy provides. So, while it may hurt to lose that true expert and settle for a "lesser" talent, ultimately it will mean that your overall team accomplishes more and reaches higher heights, and isn't that really what you want anyway?

Next Level Thinkers

Another important characteristic about your team members is that they be people who are next level thinkers. What do I mean by that? I mean that they are people who go above and beyond the normal in their thinking and come up with new and innovative ideas.

These next level thinkers are people who change the world. They are the world's inventors, explorers, dreamers and true scientists. They envision things that aren't and ask why they aren't; then they go about changing "aren't" into "are." Literally, they are the people who are responsible for every advance that humankind has made throughout the centuries.

When Chester Carlson was in the process of inventing the photocopier, he ran into a common problem that many inventors have; he ran out of money. Knowing that there was a place in the world for his invention, he went to the computer giant, IBM, seeking to sell them a portion of his invention so that he could have enough funding to finish the development of his product. He had already proven the concept, but he needed to turn it into a viable product for the marketplace.

IBM's accountants took a look at Carlson's invention and saw some potential in it. So, they investigated the financial feasibility of the product. Yet, according to their investigation, the Xerox machine wasn't worth what it would cost to finish development. Even if the Xerox took over 100% of the carbon paper market, it would take too long to cover development costs to pay for itself.

Obviously, the accountants at IBM had no idea of how to be next level thinkers. All they could see was the level where they lived; the level of the mundane. They couldn't see the change that Carlson's invention would bring to business; yet today his invention can be found in offices around the world. That was a costly error for IBM. Today, the Xerox corporation is larger and more profitable than IBM.

In reality, these next level thinkers are hard to find. Your school chum or brother-in-law probably aren't going to qualify, no matter how much they want to be part of what you're doing. If they don't have it, they just don't have it, and nothing you can do will make them into what you need.

You can't train someone how to be a next level thinker, they either are or aren't. About the most you can do is whet their appetite for those sorts of ideas. Exposing them to the work and stories of others who are next level thinkers will sometimes kick-start this sort of thinking in people, especially when they see the results of that sort of thinking. But that doesn't work with everyone. There are many people that are satisfied with the status quo and don't want anything more.

The other thing is that someone can be a next level thinker in some areas, but not in others. A lot has to do with their areas of interest. Someone who is interested in helping the poor and needy might come up with some great ideas in that area, but be incapable of thinking of a single idea for a new product, improving a product or helping make a company successful.

Herein we see that vision and next level thinking are closely tied together. Those who are committed to a vision will put much more effort into thinking about it, than those that aren't. They will also research the area, seeking to learn new things and looking for ways to apply that knowledge. Between their thinking and studying, they will be much more likely to come up with new ideas.

Of course, the problem with new ideas is that they don't all work. This is part of what keeps others from being next level thinkers. They simply don't want the risk. You see, being a next level thinker means taking risks. As Albert Einstein said, "A person who never made a mistake never tried anything new." Being a next level thinker means making yourself vulnerable. It means being willing to stake your career on an idea, and accepting whatever results fate hands you. That's too much for some people to handle. They want the security that staying within their own four walls gives them.

Those people will stay within their walls, complaining that others win big. But they aren't willing to take the risk necessary to make it big on their own. This is one of the things that sets entrepreneurs apart from others. They are willing to take risks, willing to gamble on the throw of the dice; and because they are, they tend to win big.

To those looking from the outside, that makes the entrepreneur "lucky." But while luck plays a part in their success, they largely make their own luck. Entrepreneurs aren't winners because some mysterious force called luck decides that they should be, but rather because they step out on a limb, hoping that the limb they are stepping out on is strong enough to hold them up.

On the average, those entrepreneurs fail three to four times, before they succeed; but they always succeed. You see, some people quit when they fail, but entrepreneurs fail until they succeed. They look at each failure as a chance to fall forward, not backwards. They take the time to learn the lessons from that failure, so that they can apply those to their next venture. Eventually, they learn enough lessons that they end up succeeding, rather than failing.

The good thing for you, if you're an entrepreneur, is that you're already a next level thinker. So all you have to do is find others who are like you. Often, these will be people who have an entrepreneurial spirit, but don't have the guts to step out on their own. I guess you could call them "almost entrepreneurs." So, while they never take that step to succeed on their own, they've got the right sort of attitude to be on your team and help you to become a success.

An important part of these people's character is that they see your success as their own. They aren't in competition with you, wanting to steal your success for themselves; but rather, they see their part in your success as enough for them too. Their need to succeed is fulfilled in your success, simply because they know that they are part of that success.

Recognition

Of course, these people need to be recognized and rewarded as well. Otherwise, they could lose their motivation to continue striving for the fulfillment of your vision. This is important, as your main responsibility is to direct and guide the team, acting as a mentor to it, rather than doing the work yourself.

I think the military is probably one of the greatest organizations for recognizing the contributions of its team members. The whole idea of ribbons, medals and citations is all about recognizing the contributions of outstanding team members. Interestingly enough, many of those who have received those awards, people who you and I call "heroes," don't think that they deserved the award that they received. Many of them point to others and say that those others deserve the award more than they do themselves.

This is a sign of a true team player. While they still crave the recognition that we all crave, when it is given to them, they talk about others and their contributions. That doesn't mean that they don't appreciate the recognition that they've received but rather that they are not so focused on themselves, that they have become blind to others. No, they see their own accomplishments and their own contributions, but they also see those that other team members have made.

The military also gives those who have received recognition opportunity to show it off. Actually, they go far beyond giving them that opportunity and require them to show off their

5

accomplishments. Dress uniforms are always to be worn with ribbons and qualification badges, which serve almost like a billboard of the wearer's accomplishments. Maybe all those doo-dads don't mean much to you and I, but to others in the military, it's about like reading the professional biography of those who have them.

So, how do we apply this to the business world? Simple, we follow their example. We develop awards of our own, which show the accomplishments of those who are part of our organization and which allow them some tangible reminder of our appreciation.

One company that does this fairly well is the coffee giant, Starbucks. Baristas who work for Starbucks are able to win a variety of different awards, in the form of pins and special aprons, symbolizing outstanding performance, customer appreciation and even levels of professional development. Master baristas, for example, wear distinctive black aprons, letting their co-workers and customers know that they have completed the extensive training required to be considered a Coffee Master.

While pins and aprons may not work for every case, this does give us a great image of what recognition and reward can look like. Whether it takes the form of pins, special coffee cups, a reserved parking space or a plaque on the wall, people crave these symbols of recognition. Using them is a great way of getting the most out of your team, helping motivate them to give their best and their most to fulfilling the vision.

Developing Your Team

Once you put your team together, you need to develop it. The team won't automatically meld together by leaving them in a room together. Nor will each individuals automatically develop their skills to the max. You, as a leader, are going to have to develop the team and turn it into what you needs it to be.

What we were just talking about is part of this. Recognizing accomplishment in your team is an important part of developing it; but it's not the only part. Recognition motivates, but it doesn't develop. You could say that the recognition is the carrot to get the donkey to go forward, but you need the donkey to have enough muscles to pull the cart as it goes. If your "donkey" doesn't already have the muscles you need, you're going to have to develop them.

You can break down team development into two basic areas: Developing each team member's skills and developing the team's ability to work together as a team. You have to work on both of these, but the first one you have to work on is developing the team's ability to work together as a team.

Actually, developing the team's ability to work together is more important than developing each individual's skills. This is because it is the team's ability to work together that activates the synergy we have been talking about, not individual skills. Those individual skills merely affect individual team members' ability to do their part of the project, in other words, the part which will be multiplied; but they have nothing to do with the multiplication process.

An assembly line is a fairly simple team, regardless of how complicated a product they are building. What makes it simple is that each member is doing a repetitive task. So, only a minimal amount of team building is necessary. The bulk of the multiplication comes from the form of the assembly line itself; not from the interaction of the team members.

But in cases where the team is doing something new, such as developing a new product or starting a new business, the interaction between team members becomes much more important. In these cases, you need the team members to spark ideas in each other, collaborate on parts of the project and smoothly hand-off specific tasks from one team member to another.

In this environment, how well team members know each other affects their communication, more than anything else. Considering that this sort of team activity is mostly about developing ideas and coming up with solutions to problems, communications is critical. So, you're never going to get the maximum synergy out of the team until you develop excellent communications.

One might think that developing communications is easy, but it's not. A large part of the problem is that most of us aren't good communicators, even though we think we are. Women especially think that they are great communicators, but that is only when they are communicating with other women. When it comes to communicating with men, they are just as bad as men are in communicating with women.

Part of the issue here is that we each have our own peculiarities of communication. You can think of it as if we each spoke with a different accent or we each came from a separate region of the country, where different idioms and slang terminology were used. We all think that everyone knows the same idioms and slang that we do, but they don't. They might use the same words, but have totally different meanings for them.

Much of this is the insider language that goes with any professional field. I don't care if you're talking to doctors, engineers, trash collectors or hair dressers, there's always an insider language. Some of it is the technical terminology that goes with that profession, and the rest comes out of the shortcuts that professionals develop to express their ideas within a professional field.

But your team is most likely a cross-discipline team. That means that each team member or each profession represented will have its own language, which other team members don't understand. Sadly, rather than educate fellow team members or even educating ourselves on other professional languages, we usually put up with these communications miscues and vent our frustration by talking poorly about that other professional group.

You can't have that; at least, not if you want to get the most out of your team. You've got to get everyone speaking the same language. Since they are all reluctant to learn each other's languages, the easiest solution is to develop your own language of idioms and slang, which is particular to your team.

This is actually rather easy and a lot of fun. Many of these "new words" will come out of specific events or circumstances that happen within the team. For example, you could have a situation where someone buys something for the team, let's call it a "coffee widget" without checking on the needs of everyone on the team. Once the coffee widget arrives, you find that it does everything you could ever want it to, except the one thing you need it to do... make coffee. From then on, "let's not get another coffee widget" could become part of your team's language, referring to decisions made without checking on the whole team's needs.

The truly great thing about this isn't just how it increases communications, but also how it makes everyone feel like an insider. Because you're all speaking the same insider language, you're all insiders; those who can't are outsiders. That little difference can spark the desire to develop more of your insider language, improving communications and helping everyone feel like they are part of the team.

The other thing needed for developing the team is for everyone to know each other's capabilities. I suppose you could think I mean knowing the skills and education listed on each person's resume, but that's not really what I'm talking about. We all expect an engineer to know engineering and a marketing specialist to know marketing. But there are many aspects to engineering and many specialties in that field. Likewise, there are many aspects and specializations in marketing too. Just because someone is a marketing expert, doesn't mean they know social media marketing, nor does being a mechanical engineer make someone a great auto mechanic.

The funny part of this is that we all think that we know what other professionals do, but we basically have no idea about it. Oh, we know the broad strokes, but we don't understand anything of the details. We especially don't understand the process they use to get to the finished result. That's okay to a point, but it can cause massive misunderstandings.

But even learning the details of another's profession doesn't mean that you understand what the individual is capable of doing. We all have a list of skills that have nothing to do with our jobs. Maybe one team member is an amateur photographer and another builds furniture as a hobby. There might be an artist in your team or a near-Olympic level athlete. Those skills won't show up on a resume, but they could be highly valuable. That athlete could become the center of your product advertising, photographed by the team member who knows photography, on a stage built by the furniture maker and in front of a background painted by the artist, who also does the ad layout.

Wow, we just put together an advertisement with our own team's talent, instead of having to go outside and look for it all. While that may not be necessary for your team, unless your team members know each other's skills and capabilities, there isn't any chance of accomplishing that sort of collaboration.

Perhaps these sorts of skills won't play much of a role in your team's work; but if your team doesn't know one another well enough to know about those things, there's no way that it can happen. So, it's worth investing the time in getting to know one another that well, permitting those opportunities to be created.

There's one other thing that your team members need to know about each other, that's each person's "soft skills." What do I mean by that? Those are the job-related skills that we all learn, which help us to be good workers. This broad category includes such things as our punctuality, work ethic, organizational skills and work habits.

Knowing each other's work habits and personality can help to avoid conflict in the team. If you have a team member who is a late riser, for example, and sounds like a grizzly bear until they have their second cup of coffee, it probably won't be a good idea to schedule a meeting or a brainstorming session with them, early in the morning. Better to do it after lunch, when they are probably more awake, more amicable and thinking clearly.

Okay, so now you've got your team together and everyone is communicating with each other. They've learned about each other's skills, hobbies and personal habits. The team is starting to flow together, creating ideas and putting them together. Now it's time to start working on individual development of the various team members.

None of us are where we need to be, professionally speaking. We need to increase our knowledge and improve our skills. Actually, this should be an important part of any professional's life, throughout their career. I don't know about you, but I really wouldn't want to see a doctor who wasn't making the effort to be up to date on all the latest developments in their field. Actually, I could say the same for a number of different professional fields, from engineering to marketing.

Your team members come to you with a set of skills and knowledge. But more importantly than that, they come with an entrepreneurial attitude, if you've selected them right. Even so, that doesn't mean that they have all the skills or all the knowledge you need. Granted, you probably looked for that in the selection process, but they probably still aren't perfect.

Okay, that's really no big deal. It's always possible for people to learn new things. In fact, it's desirable for them to do so. Not only does it help them with their professional development, but it helps you and your company, by having people who are more capable.

We were talking earlier about The Home Depot and their customer service. One of the things that makes them so good at customer service is that they hire people who are knowledgeable about the various building trades to work in their stores. But that doesn't mean that those people know everything. In fact, they really don't expect their new employees to know everything. They train them.

Home Depot has a rather extensive training program for new employees, one which takes a year to complete. While their associates start working the floor long before completing it, they continue learning while they are working. Then, once they become fully trained in one building specialty, they start learning another. Their education continues, making them more valuable to the company and to their customers.

Investing in the professional development of your team members always pays off. The new skills they learn help make them more efficient on the job, as well as increasing the range of what they can do for the team. Classes, seminars and training sessions aren't a means of stealing from the work day, but rather a means of adding to what can be accomplished on future work days. That's where they pay off.

Some leaders take a passive approach to personal development of their team members, waiting for them to request permission to attend a training event. But it's much better for a leader to be seeking out those opportunities and suggesting them to their employees. Not only does that help to fill in gaps in the   team's overall knowledge and ability, but it's a great way of showing team members that you care about them as individuals, and their future.

Leading Your Team

I know I said it before, but I need to say it again; your job isn't to do the work of the team, but rather to put the team together and lead it. The whole reason you have a team is so that they will do the work, ultimately multiplying your ability to accomplish your goals. When you do your job as leader correctly, then your team is able to do their jobs correctly.

Whole books have been written about leadership, so I'm not going to attempt to give you a lesson on leadership in these few short pages. But there are a few important points which I think tie in with the other things we've talked about and which you need to pay special attention to.

First of all, leaders and managers are not the same. If you try to manage your team, you may as well give up now. Managers run bureaucracies, not teams; so managing your team will only turn it into a bureaucracy. That's not what you want and that's not going to accomplish your goal.

Let me say something here; bureaucracies never invent anything new. New ideas aren't created by some mandate from upper management or by some department of controlling people. New ideas come from mavericks; people who think outside the box and break the rules. If you want something new out of your team, than you need to fight tooth and nail to keep it from even remotely turning into a bureaucracy.

As a leader, you have to stay out in front. I love the image of an infantry platoon leader going "over the top" and yelling to his troops, "Follow me!" That's probably the ultimate in leadership and a perfect example of the leadership you need to have. You need to be that one out in front; setting the direction; establishing the vision and saying "Follow me!"

The big risk in not being out in front is that the team ends up deviating from the chosen path and going the wrong way. Granted, some deviations can actually improve what you're trying to do; but those are in the minority. Without a leader out in front, taking a good look at those detours and making decisions about them, it's all too easy for the team to end up going down a detour, not even realizing that the detour is a different path than they want to go.

How can you tell if a detour is good or bad? It's simple actually. All you have to do is compare it to the vision. If it is included within the vision or can help you accomplish the vision, then it's good. But if it is nothing more than a distraction, which takes you in a different direction, then it's bad.

Since you're the one who came up with the vision, you are the world's number one expert on it. So, you are the person who is best equipped to ensure that the team stays on target and is working towards that vision. Just because your team members have caught the vision, doesn't mean they are experts. They could have a distorted idea of the vision, and even the slightest distortion could create a huge detour.

Being in front also gives you the ability to set the pace. That's extremely useful, but you have to be sensitive to those who are following you. Setting a pace that they can't keep up with only separates you from them. But setting a pace that causes them to strive to keep up can accomplish a lot.

A true leader understands this instinctively, because a true leader is always focused on their team, rather than on themselves. They aren't looking for a personal win, but rather a team win. So, they concentrate on their team members, helping them reach their full potential. Through that, they end up bringing their team to its full potential.

Basically, everything we've talked about in this chapter has been about leading that team. From the very beginning, when you choose your team members, you're leading them. You're leading them both on a corporate level (as a group) and individually. Recognition and working on their professional development are both parts of leading them individually. But they also have an impact on the larger goal of leading the team.

In a sense, being a leader is more about being a mentor, than anything else. You become that trusted advisor and trainer for your team members, working with each one individually, for the betterment of your team. Part of this is helping them grow as professionals and individuals, but another is advising them on their part of the team's effort.

There's one thing that being a manager and being a leader have in common, although they aren't done in the same way. That's spending a lot of time in meetings. The big difference is that managers spend a lot of time in formal meetings, where information is disseminated and decisions are avoided. But a leader spends a lot of time meeting with individuals and small sub-teams, discussing the project, the approach being taken, brainstorming, seeking ideas and ultimately making decisions.

You see, as the leader, you need to be involved in every aspect of what your team is doing. It doesn't matter whether you are an expert in a particular area or not, you need to be there. Nobody can be an expert in everything and you shouldn't try to give your team a snow job by pretending you are. But you should be interested in everything that's going on.

Once again, this is about keeping the team on track. By meeting with individuals and sub-groups, you are able to check what is being done and make sure it is within the scope of the vision. At the same time, you have a part in the decisions being made, ensuring that they are the right ones. Since you are part of those decisions, it eliminates the tendency to point fingers and fix blame when something goes wrong. Instead, you look to solve the problem, along with the team members who were part of that decision.

This can make a huge difference. Nobody likes to be reminded of their failures or have everyone pointing their finger at them. But most true professionals want another crack at solving a problem that has defeated them. So, by making decisions together with team members, another thing you do is to really motivate them when it's time to take that second crack at the problem.

These personal meetings become a great opportunity for mentoring. It is through them that you can share your understanding and knowledge, better than in any other way. At the same time, you can talk to each team member about their contribution, how to improve it and find out what that team member needs, so that they can do their best.

Mentoring is rewarding work, but the greatest reward is the results it will have on your project. Yes, you'll see results in the individual; but you'll also see results in your team's abilities, your team's cohesiveness and your team's work.

When all is said and done, building that team and the time you invest in training and mentoring will pay off handsomely. Maybe you won't see your personal productivity increase; but you'll see a whole lot more accomplished and accomplished well. A lot more than you could ever expect to do on your own. Isn't that why you want a team in the first place?

Contact Info for Chis 'mere Mallard

Chismere Mallard Has a wealth of knowledge in a variety of disciplines. He has the insight of someone that has been there and is willing to make sure you have the tools to go there as well. After graduation from the University of Texas Pan-American with a BA is Sociology, Chis'mere managed a personal trainer business. It was there that he discovered the joy of empowering others to succeed. He became more than a fitness trainer; encouraging people to not only succeed in their fitness goals but in their personal goals for their lives. This passion has led him to seek out others and encourage them.

Today, Chis'mere owns and manages CLS Devices, LLC, representing several multi-million dollar companies, as well as his own life-coaching and inspirational speaking company, Chis'mere Mallard, LLC. He can be reached at...

Chrismeremallard23@gmail.com

www.chismeremallard.com

He is available for Coaching, Keynote Speaking, Conferences, Seminars, panels, webinars and presentations

Chapter 3: Association Brings about Collaboration

By: Johnny "MACKnificent" Mack

There are many reasons people fail to finish things. One obvious reason is associations. It's been said many times that your success will be determined by the people you associate with and the books you read. Let's look at the first criterion, your associations.

You surround yourself with people for myriad reasons. You like some of them, some of them like you. You work with or attend church with others. Sometimes you associate with a person because a friend introduced him or her. Other times it is because you are in similar groups.

The bottom line is most people have associations due to reasons other than personal choice.

If you look back over the group of friends you have. Most of them were sort of just dropped in your lap. When you really think it through, you did not consciously decide that each person would be your friend.

You have degrees of friends. Some are close, others are closer, and some are just associates. When you consider your success is determined by those that you associate with on a regular bases, it may well be worth evaluating why you have certain people as friends.

The principle is this, if you have a friend that is lazy or negative or too satisfied with mediocrity, one of two things happens. You either mirror those same traits or you influence that friend to step up his game and become more like you. The effort required to step up your game is so hard most people just acquiesce and default to the lower level.

When there are so many other important things to do and consider, the prospect of influencing a friend to be better is daunting at best. So rather than risk the friendship or an unpleasant confrontation, most people just go along to get along. This leads to vacillating between things.

You on the one hand know that their behavior is counter to what you have decided to do with your life. Yet you justify it as okay in order to not lose a friend or get into a confrontation with one.

The end result is that association adds to the demise of your best actions.

Instead of your doing that extra or pushing harder, you go along with your friend (who has no desire to go higher, he is happy just to make it) soon you are okay with mediocre and do just enough to get by.

Whereas you see your life in the lens of Focus and Intention, now you are dis-focused and your intention has waned. This is in large part due to your adopting the actions and activities of your friend.

If you are to reach the goals you have set for yourself, it is imperative that you surround yourself with likeminded people. Positive people influence you to do positive things. Conversely, negative people influence you to do negative things.

If the five people you associate with are primarily negative, you will find yourself starting and not completing things. You will see yourself as a failure or 'so-so' at best. The effort required to begin and complete a task will be robbed from you.

You will find it easy to quit because negative people quit and blame it on circumstance, situation, and difficulty.

You must find positive likeminded people that have your best interests at heart. You must surround yourself with **'Focused Finishers'** that believe in themselves and you.

Your network must consist of winners and beginners. Those who know what they desire and are willing to take the extra steps to reach them. Those that do not fit in that category will be like dead weight on you, dragging you down and preventing you from having the vision of completion.

Often times it is family that drains you. They smother you with the spirit of familiarity. They remind you of what you have accomplished and make you believe that you are average and ordinary. Family makes you confront the demons of your past and convince you that you should not even try. Family justifies failure and incompletion. They recommend you abandon this task before it drains you and brands you a failure.

Family tells you to save face by not doing things that will expose your inability to do them. So you end up folding once again and look back at even more attempts that met with failure and no finish.

Let's stop right here and imagine a situation. You and your two best friends are discussing an issue. Each of your friends are opinionated. Friend #1 is passionate about a certain neighborhood. Friend #2 is less so and suggests you just make up your own mind. You have an option and would like to move in a different direction. Friend #1 begins to tell you why he is so against this specific area.

You listen and begin to have doubts about the area you have considered moving to. Friend #2 is quiet which makes you think he feels the same way as friend #1. You listen intently to Friend #1 and soon you decide to take the advice of that person due to your association with him and the passion of his presentation.

This is exactly how most decisions are made. Not with reasoned approach or scholarly discourse, but by listening to the passionate advice of a close friend. In most cases the friend just gives an opinion. Not that he is even qualified to speak on the issue; he just shares his or her opinion.

I sold cars for many years, in many instances a purchase decision was made by a so called expert. A family member or friends set themselves up to be the quasi expert and rather than risk ridicule, the buyer would run every car purchase by them.

He may or may not have been able to get a decent deal for himself. It doesn't matter, the fact that they were able to become the designated authority gives them responsibility and clout.

Many a person has made decisions based on information or influence from this self proclaimed expert. Influenced by this person, many people cede their authority to another in an effort to be included, accepted or not judged.

To someone on the sidelines, it may look as if that person is being taken advantage of or at best being led wrong, but that is the power of those in our network. We give over to crowd confidence and group think.

It's easier and less demanding to give control of our thoughts and decisions to another or a group, than to take full responsibly for it ourselves. If we make a choice on our own the group will laugh at it, or ridicule it and that is a worse fate to some people than physical pain. Disassociation or ostracism is a form of punishment and public disapproval.

Whereas some people could care less what others think of them, there are those who care very much.

It is that ceding of power that makes your associations so dangerous. You have given control of your thinking over to someone else. In the long run this influence of action causes some to not do what is necessary to complete task.

There are myriad reasons why the mind shuts downs and ceases the completion process. I contend that friends and associates and even strangers can have this affect on us. Rather than disappoint or anger these outside influences, many people will abandon activity that may invoke disapproval from these 'experts'.

Your Associations can be Lethal or Leveraging.

Those that surround themselves with positive goal getters soon find themselves in that mindset. They strive to be winners and get satisfaction out of completion. It is those that find themselves in the company of losers or cowards at best, that are unable to finish.

The company you keep will decide many things about and for you. One of the easiest ways to begin the process of completion is to limit those in your circle that are negative, lazy or inactive. Those types of associates will pull you away from activity in your best interest.

You must have the mindset that completing tasks and goals is important.

Once that is your paradigm, you will resist anything or anyone that tries to dissuade you from that process. It's not always easy to remove yourself from family or close friends. But once you recognize them as time wasters or dream killers you must jettison them.

The familiar feeling of comfort that you get from being around them is also the same feeling of distraction you receive when you consciously or unconsciously find yourself not finishing another task.

It is very unsettling to come to the conclusion that a valued friend or loving family member is toxic to your success cycle. The truth must not only be told, it must be accepted.

Once the brain has found an escape from the effort required to complete a task, it will take it. That means it's more comfortable to resist the effort to do what is required.

Your associations, more than anything will be the source of resistance regarding your doing what you need to do.

Take time today to evaluate everyone you allow to be in your circle of influence. If they are not encouraging you to do your best and make the extra effort, you need to decide if they are of any value to you... I know this may sound harsh but your very success depends on it.

Most of your associations are there for their sake not yours. They are looking for likeminded individuals to give credibility to their lack of performance. They want you to validate the fact that they are slackers or at best 'average'. Any attempt you make to be a finisher or a completer makes them look average and ordinary. That is okay as long as you and everyone else are in the same boat. Once you start rowing toward the sea of success you remind them of their lack and averageness. You have to find a likeminded group of people to associate with. They must be of the mindset that success is not only possible, it is priority. You can then feed off their enthusiasm and focus.

Those that celebrate your success will cause you to want to succeed more. Those that criticize your effort to succeed will become the stumbling blocks on your road to winning. Stop letting them slow you down.

Recap

The people you network with and associate with will determine if you win or lose. If you find yourself in the company of winners and they are encouraging you to win, chances are you will be a winner. Conversely when you find yourself in the company of losers and complainers and drainers you will not complete much and what you do finish will be dismissed as invaluable. Make sure you surround yourself with the right kind of people and read the right kind of books and experience the right kind of media….your 'good life' may depend on it

Contact Info for Johnny MACKnificent Mack

Johnny "MACKnificent" Mack is the author of 15 Best sellers. He has been a committed writer for over 40 years and began publishing 5 years ago. Once he discovered the intricate world of self publishing he saw a significant need in the arena. After over 10,000 hours of study and practice he began helping other self publish their works. This lead to the establishment of the Self Published Authors Network. He has coached and help 25 other authors became published authorizing his signature ABS Model (Automatic Best Seller). SPAN is now working with some of the top transformational thought leaders in the industry. He can be reached at..

askjmack2@gmail.com
www.SPANBOSS.com
www.SelfPublishedAuthorsNetwork.com

He is available for Coaching, Keynote Speaking, Conferences, Seminars, panels, webinars and presentations

Chapter 4: Collaboration Makes your Why Work
By: Edward C. Williams

A t some point you are going to have to come to terms with your life. The question is will they be your terms? Was it your life? Why are you doing what you are doing? Let's jump right into it, there is no more time to waste. There are so many things we do every day that we don't have a clue why. What are the end results? Many times we start things but what was our why? What I am about to share with you is intended to do few things.

First it is to get you to take an honest look at yourself, to get you to start believing in yourself, to get you to act on that belief and finally to let you know why you should. I truly believe every one of us are here for a purpose I refuse to believe that God put anyone here just to fill space. That means if you reading this, it is meant to be and this message is for you. I want you to ask yourself three questions. Am I living the life I really want to live? Am I doing the things I really want to do? If I died today can I say like Paul the apostle said "I have fought a good fight' if the answer to those questions is no, then you are reading just what you need to right now.

Like so many others, I was going through my life with no direction, no purpose and no passion. I did whatever the day brought me to do, I followed people who had nowhere to go. I spent my time talking to people who had nothing to talk about. I worked at jobs I didn't like with people I didn't like and who more than likely didn't like me. I lived in fear which in turn made me a victim, and because I was not living within my own power I allowed myself to get sucked into the lives and drama of other people. I thank God he opened my eyes before it was too late, and it happened with one word, Why? Why are you living like you are living? Why are you not living the life you want to live? Why are you here in a state of mental anguish?

Now don't misunderstand me I don't claim to be a guru or have all the answers. I am a work in progress, I am nowhere near where I want to be, but as the saying goes, I thank God, I am not where I used to be. What about you? Again are you living your life, or the life society has dealt you? Are you pursuing your dreams or just walking in the shadows of someone else's nightmare? Are you spending your days with peace and bliss or with heartache and misery? It is time to stop, it is time to embrace your greatness and walk boldly into your life!

What is your bliss? What makes you happy? What would you do if you didn't have bills, fear, and knew you couldn't fail? What is your dream? Have you taken the time to discover your T.A.G, (Talents, Abilities and Gifts) We are all born with our own T.A.G. No one can do what you do, the way you do it, no one else can sing your song, write your book, start your business, dance your dance, and most of all live your life.

There are a number of reasons why people don't pursue their dreams or their passions but the biggest one is fear. Fear has killed more dreams than all diseases in the world. Most people are just simply afraid to step out and trust themselves I know because I was one of them. I had all these great ideas, this great passion to help people through motivation and inspiration. To write books and do seminars and workshops, but out of fear of failure and being talked about I stayed in my comfort zone of average and ordinary which in itself was a failure and people talked about me anyway. So I made up my mind to go after my dream and pursue my passion if I fail at the very least it will be at something I love doing and as for people talking, they are going to do that anyway.

There is greatness in you, you are more powerful than you will ever know. There isn't a dream, an idea or vision that God didn't put in your heart that he can't put in your hands, all you have to do is believe. I have heard people say I believe in God but I don't know if I can do it. Listen, believing in God, but not in yourself is self-defeating. God works through you, what good is God's light in you, if you are too afraid to let it shine. Fear is crippling, it puts us in a mental state of inaction.

We don't do the things we know we need to do out of fear of failure, fear of the unknown. We choose to stay where we are no matter how damaging or unhappy we are because we are comfortable there and afraid to step out on faith. We stay in dead end unfulfilling jobs, too afraid to start our own business or seek out better opportunities, out of fear of loss. So many people stay in toxic unhappy relationships out of fear of being alone and talked about.

It's like someone has put you on a boat and the boat for whatever reason got hung up and stopped just offshore of your destiny. You can see the shore but you will have to get out of the boat to get there, but the water looks deep. There are other people on the boat telling you just wait help is coming, someone will save us. There you sit rocking in the boat riding the waves of mediocrity sometimes up, sometimes down but going nowhere. Rocking 5 years, 10 years, 20 years, 30 years, when are you going to get off the boat!!? The water isn't as deep as you think.

The next big reason is they don't have a **why.** They haven't found a cause bigger than themselves, money, or just getting through the day to live for. In order to live a worthy and purpose filled life you must have a why? You need a cause that will benefit and aid others. Some people use a forgettable past, their children, a lost or a life changing experience as their *why* to do something or make a change. Your **why,** if it is big enough will keep you going when things get tough. It will push you pass what others see as breaking points. Your **why** is your key to opening the door past your limitations. What is your **why**?

Each and every one of us are here for a purpose, and in our hearts we know this and desire to live that purpose. But, yet so many of us are not. Why, I believe it is because we never came into the knowledge of who we really are, one author wrote " the two most important day of your life is the day you were born and the day you discover **why** you were born.

Well Edward, some of you may be asking what is your **why**? Thanks for asking. Actually I have two. The first is I wanted to live a life worthy of the gift of life I was given. If God thought enough of me to bless me with this life, I should think enough of myself to live it the best I can. Second my two sons, I wanted to leave something behind other than a name. They need to be able to say YEAH my dad did that!

Let me sum this up for you. If you don't start looking pass your past and get a bigger vision of who you are and what you can do. If you don't give yourself a **WHY** to succeed, not only are you cheating yourself but we all miss out. We will never read the book you didn't write, or listen to the songs you never sang, we will never hang the art you never created. We can never share in the love you didn't give nor can we thank God for the life your never lived.

There is so much more to you, you have so much more to offer this life. There is greatness in you. You have the essence of God himself in you, the almighty I AM therefore you are.

You are powerful, you are a conqueror, you are a champion, you are greatness. Embrace your greatness and walk boldly into your life. However, this will not be an easy journey, you are going to have to make some major changes and some of them are going to take time.

You are going have to let some people go and this will be hard, the negative, draining and toxic people will be easy, but the good friend who just won't get where you are going will have to be left behind. Anything that no longer serves you and helping you reach the shore must be removed and replaced. The first step is changing your way of thinking, you now must start focusing on what you what, not on what you don't.

You must focus on where you want to go, not on where you are. You must focus on where you are going to, not on what you are going through. Then you must start believing in yourself. You can't achieve anything unless you believe you can. Henry Ford said "if you believe you can or if you believe you can't you are right." As God himself tells us whatsoever a man believeth in his heart so is he. Then you must act on that belief.

I have no idea what your dreams and passions are or your purpose in life, but I do know this, if you are still reading this, you and I have one thing in common, we know we can be more. We have greatness in us and it is time to embrace it. Stop living small, stop living in fear, stop going to places you shouldn't go, stop chasing people you don't need to be chasing, stop living your life in someone else's mind. Get around people who empower, motivate and inspire you. Read books that will grow you. Set goals that will challenge you. There is greatness in you. I repeat... there is greatness in you, embrace it!

A final word, as I mentioned earlier, this won't be easy, there are going to be some trials, some disappointments, some heartache and some pain but here is the deal...it will be worth it. Understand this, you can live life in one of two ways. You can live it making things happen for you, or live it allowing things to happen to you.

Embrace your greatness and walk boldly into your life.

I know all that sounds easy right? But oh God it is not, so let me share with you 10 steps to help you step into your greatness and become the person you know in your heart you should be. Than you can tell them *WHY* you did it.

Step #1

Decide What You Want!. Most people can tell you what they don't want, but they have a hard time deciding what they do want. How can you have a dream come true if you don't have a dream? If you don't have anywhere to go, you are already there!

Step#2

Write it down.... in order for your goals to be effective, they must be written. Ideas that remains in the mind will become only wishes.

Step#3

Read your Goals 3 times a Day.....Once you write your goals, then you must read them three times daily. Once in the morning to get you started, once again during the day to keep you focused and once before you go to bed.

Step#4

Set a Date....If you don't set a date, you will procrastinate. You must set a date and make yourself accountable to that date. It will help you to get someone you trust to be an accountability partner.

Step#5

Meditate.....Most people are too busy from the time they get up, till the time they go to bed. They are so busy, they don't take time to think and be at peace. Take a few minutes every day to meditate and calm yourself. Think about your goals and dreams. Your mind will to go to work on how to make those dreams come true.

Steps#6

Dream and Imagine..... Use your imagination. You must see it in the mind before you can achieve it. See yourself in the house you want, or the car you want to drive, make your own bank statement with the balance you want. Once you see it, you create an emotional connection!

Step#7

Take Action..... Now get off your butt and go do something. you need a plan of action; it doesn't need to be in detail but it does need to get you from point A to point B. You heard it before" Plan your work and then work your plan"

Step#8

Do 3 things a day toward your goals.... Develop a habit of doing something every day toward your dreams. Write a letter, make a phone call, send an e-mail, learn something new.

Step#9

Act as though you already have it.... Therefore, I say unto you, what things so ever ye desire, when ye pray, believe that ye receive (them) and ye shall have (them).... enough said...

Step#10

Stay Positive!..This is one of the hardest things to do, because the first thing most people hear in the morning is bad news. We hear who got killed overnight, robbed or raped. We are told how bad the economy is and how bad it is all over. Make a commitment to start your day with something positive. Read or listen to something positive in the first few minutes of your day.

One last thing if you have read this and still think you can't do it or have nothing to offer. If you still somehow think no one will benefit or be blessed by your achieving a dream. I leave you with this short story.

I call it The Triumph of a Loser

When he was little all the other kids call him Sparky, after a comic book horse named Spark Plug. Sparky never did shake that nickname. School was all but impossible for Sparky he failed every subject in the 8th grade. Throughout his youth Sparky was awkward socially, he was not actually disliked by the others children, no one really cared that much. He was amazed if any of them would speak to him outside of school hours. No way to tell how he would have done at dating all of his school years Sparky never asked a girl out, he was sure they would laugh and say no.

Sparky was loser and everyone knew it so he just decided to roll with it. However, there was one thing Sparky knew he could do, draw, Sparky was proud of his on art work, of course no one else liked it.

In his senior year of high school, he submitted some drawing for his school yearbook, of course they were rejected. Although this was very painful, he was so convinced of his artistic ability that he decided to become a professional artist.

Upon graduating from high school he sent a letter to Walt Disney studios and was asked to send some samples and a cartoon was suggested. Sparky drew the proposed cartoon and some others, he spent a lot of time on them. The reply from Disney came, once again Sparky was rejected another loss for the loser.

So, Sparky decided to write his own story in cartoon, about the little boy loser, The story would become famous all over the world, for the little boy who failed every subject in the 8th grade, and whose work was turned down again and again, was Charles Monroe "Sparky" Schultz. He created the Peanuts Gang and the little boy whose kite would never fly Charlie Brown. Believe in yourself even when no one else does and never give up on your dream.

Info on Edward C. Williams

Edward C. Williams is a mastermind specialist. He is the Founder of the Power Life Group. His witty and wise adages have helped his clients achieve Clarity, composure and conviction. His weekly Power talks program is the talk of the town. Edward has the enviable ability to look in your soul and see the side of you that you thought no one could. Edward is currently the author of two best sellers, with a spin off series of his popular Powerlife slated to become a chicken soup for the soul type of branding. Mr. Williams is single and can be contacted at ...

williams.Powerlife@gmail.com
williamsPowerlife@gmail.com

He is available for Coaching, Keynote Speaking, Conferences, Seminars, panels, webinars and presentations

Chapter 5: Collaboration: Why is the new What

By Daryl Fletcher

I n 1982 the Los Angeles Lakers drafted a 6'9 Small Forward from the Tar Heels of the University of North Carolina. This small forward was selected to the Lakers not only because he was a great player but also because he was a great leader. This small forward was a part of a powerhouse trio in the collegiate level. That powerhouse consisted of James Worthy, Sam Perkins and Michael Jordan. The Lakers drafted James Worthy. As a junior power forward, Worthy was the leading scorer of a Tar Heels NCAA Championship. A consensus first team All-American, Worthy shared College Player of the Year honors with Virginia Cavalier's Ralph Sampson.

He dominated the 1982 championship game against the Georgetown Hoyas, sealing the Tar heels' 63–62 victory by intercepting an inadvertent pass thrown by Hoya point guard Fred Brown with just seconds remaining. His shooting, 28 points and 4 rebounds capped a standout performance throughout the NCAA tournament, earning him it's Most

Outstanding Player award. Worthy was proven leader so he knew he could play in the next level professionally. He was the go to guy for the Tar heels and was drafted as the overall pick in the 1982 NBA draft.

That same year the Lakers had already won the NBA championship. Magic Johnson and Kareem Abdul-Jabbar led that team. Johnson would receive the reward of Most Valuable player that year. Magic being one of the leaders of the Laker squad had a system of building camaraderie within the team of hanging out, going to movies and doing things together as a team. Worthy was quoted as saying "all he wanted to do was to home in on his talent and make his contribution to the team". He didn't want to listen to anyone say let's get together and go out as a team.

He would listen to coaches and owners but listening to someone on the same court was difficult for him to do. He just wanted to play his game and make a contribution to the team on the court. He didn't understand why it was in important for him to do things with the team outside the game. He questioned why any of those activities were important. This questioning created friction between Worthy and Johnson. Very few people knew what was going on inside the locker room however there was a problem brewing that would challenge the ability for the team to collaborate. This friction would go on for a few years. In the following 2 seasons after Worthy was drafted the Lakers would not win a championship. It was during this time the "Why" behind the "What" was being challenged. Even though James Worthy was a really good player and known leader; he was also a lone wolf.

He liked doing things alone and not collaborating with his teammates off the court. It took a few years for Worthy to understand that Magic Johnson was the true leader of the Los Angeles Lakers team. Even with them winning one championship together there was still friction. This friction created rumors and ideas of Worthy being traded. This was something that he didn't want. He finally had to realize why off court participation was important for what the team needed to sustain more championships.

When you understand your "why", your "what" becomes clearer. When you meet someone for the first time, one of the first questions that is asked is "What do you do?" But the real question is "Why." Why did you choose your career? Why did you select your college? Why did you select the car you drive? These are questions we rarely ask ourselves. But when you begin to ask yourself the Why's to life the What's will become easier to accomplish. When it comes to business and entrepreneurship why is it important to collaborate? Many people have a challenging time when they first start out because they don't want anyone to steal their ideas, products or services.

I believe that it is important for one to protect themselves when they are starting out but there also comes a point where you are going to need some form of partnership. There is an old saying that says: "If you want to go fast go alone, but if you want to go far go together. So as you are on the journey to accomplishment and achieving, understanding your why will shape the decisions that you need to make along the way. If you're anything like James Worthy you might be challenged and desire to be a lone wolf. You might be a person that wants to say "I did it on my own." There is nothing wrong with wanting to do things alone. But why do it alone if you could do it with someone.

Human beings were not designed to be alone. Every human being is a product of collaboration. Your mother and father got together and collaborated to get you here. Whether they still like each other or not the thing is that for a few moments in time there was a collaboration that produced you. Even if you may think you are a mistake, you are still here for a purpose.

I hear my colleague Dr. Ed Womack say this all the time. "There are two important dates for a person; the day that they were born and the day that they understand why. If you would look within yourself right now you may begin to realize that what you do is not as important as why you do it.

I first heard of the story of Magic and Worthy's friction from my friend Billy Thompson that used to play with the Lakers during the "Showtime Era." I found it hard to believe that my childhood basketball hero Magic Johnson and James Worthy didn't get along. When you saw them on the court it was poetry in motion. On the court they had a common goal and a common enemy. The common goal was to win and the common enemy was the other team. Off the court it was a struggle to get along . When James Worthy heard about the possibility of being traded to another team he looked within himself acknowledged that his inability to grasp the "why" was about to alter is path.

He made the decision to meet with Magic Johnson for lunch one day and they began to connect the dots of why the off court participation with his teammates was so important in accomplishing the goals of winning championships. In researching this story from multiple sources I was able to pick out 4 principles that I believe James Worthy had to come to grips with:

- **Acknowledgement of the Why**
- **Adjustment to the Why**
- **Agreement to the Why**
- **Action to make the Why happen**

"Acknowledgement to weakness is the first step to gaining strength"

There are three things that James Worthy had to acknowledge the first thing he had to acknowledge was not the leader of the Lakers as he was in University North Carolina. the second thing he had to acknowledge is that his method of doing things was not getting him the results that he needed and that the team wanted. Thirdly he had to acknowledge is there was a method in place and he had to acknowledge that method was the best method for that team

When we look at the power of collaboration there are a few questions that come to mind. but when he did the result was a championships in 1985, 87 & 88.

Info on Daryl Fletcher

Daryl Fletcher is a social engineer. He has the clear insight to direct marketing to where it needs to be focused. He works with business owners and entrepreneurs to get the right grip. Daryl loves nothing better than working with youth (Especially African American Male Youth.) Daryl graduated from Florida Memorial college with a degree in Business Administration. He is the Founder of Dynamic Lifestyle and is also the Author a just published book entitled ***Disgustingly Beautiful*** (Available on Amazon.) Daryl is not only a speaker, coach, Youth Empowerment Specialist, and entrepreneur, he has a genuine love for people. Daryl can be reached at....

info@DarylFletcherSpeaker.com 404-807-7624

www.Daryl FletcherSpeaks.com

He is available for Coaching, panels, webinars and Keynote Speaking, Conferences, Seminars, presentations

Chapter 6: Be UNSTOPPABLE with Collaboration
By: Terrance "The Unstoppable Coach" Leftridge

When I think of collaboration, I can't help but thinking about what has occurred with the "Men of Vision" over the last 18 months. This journey was first born out of one man's vision. One man's vision in the Midwest not knowing that this vision was also being birthed and branded in another man's vision in New Mexico. Yet another man's vision in Dallas and two powerful brothers also had that same vision in Atlanta Georgia. We were all looking to be able to go farther faster.

We came together as five individuals all destined for greatness within our own businesses. But we had a greater vision. A vision of not seeing other men, especially African Americans remain stuck in competition when we knew we could go farther faster through collaboration.

We all had a desire for examples of what men can do when they put their minds to being greater with each other than without. So on one Sunday night in November 2014, the "Men of Vision" came together to start on that journey of showing the world what collaboration really looks like.

And since then, we have all seen exponential growth not only in the "Men of Vision" movement, but also in our individual endeavors. We've become individual best-selling authors; we have been able to increase our speaking events, and we have name recognition across the country as men who are doing great things together.

It has by no means been easy. Whenever you bring a number of individuals together with their individual personalities, their individual beliefs, and their individual ways of doing things, there is bound to be some friction. With any endeavor if it was easy, no one would do it.

What I would like to share with you over this chapter are **"REASONS WHY"** you should engage in the **"Power of Collaboration"** if you plan to go into business. I call it the **"B.C.A's. of Collaboration!"** Throughout this chapter, I'm going to reference what we do in the "Men of Vision" so that the people understand how powerful this collaboration is.

I want to share with you through my journey and the journey of the "Men of Vision" how we have received BENEFITS from collaboration; received needed COACHING and COUNSEL as a result of collaboration and have received new levels of ACCOUNTABILITY through collaboration.

DEFINITION:

So exactly what is collaboration? Collaboration is defined when two or more entities come together as individual components to create a collective greater product, service or thing. Collaboration is a meeting of the minds. Collaborative success is the culmination of more than one great idea coming together to make a greater idea reality.

Collaboration can be found in many different segments of life. It is done daily in Corporate America where groups work together exchanging ideas and brainstorming on mutual ways to achieve common goals. It is seen in the small business segment work, like minded businesses come together and leverage their expertise and contacts to serve more people together than they could ever serve by themselves. Thought Leaders, Speakers and Coaches all across the country lend their Talents, Abilities and Gifts to one another in a collaborative spirit at conferences and events.

It has by no means been easy. Whenever you bring a number of individuals together with their individual personalities, their individual beliefs, and their individual ways of doing things, there is bound to be some friction. With any endeavor if it was easy, no one would do it. But collaboration causes you to check your ego at the door. MOV member Edward C. Williams sums it up this way: "It's not about ME-Go; it's about where WE-Go, so check your Ego!" So let's talk more about the BENEFITS of collaboration.

BENEFITS of Collaboration:

Collaboration creates a new spirit of understanding about your role within the collaboration and how the collaboration can lead to the greater good of the group as well as you individually. It is because of that greater benefit, that greater expectation, that collaboration works in most relationships as well as in most businesses.

If you read any of the popular business magazines like Entrepreneur or Forbes, you'll notice that business leaders, academics and researchers who study entrepreneurship recognize collaboration and information sharing as important as more obvious skills such as opportunity recognition and determination. Entrepreneurs see the value in collaborating with others in order to get things done faster and more efficiently. With the advent of email, file sharing, High speed internet, Google hangouts, Go-to-Meeting and other video conferencing applications, the ability to collaborate across the globe has never been easier.

Entrepreneurs value speed and ease of access. When you recognize you can go farther faster when you collaborate with like-minded individuals using today's technological advances, then it's a no-brainer.

Sharing the Load is another benefit of collaboration. I am reminded of a proverb that the "Men of Vision" often use as one of our tenets. It simply says "If you want to go fast, go alone; if you want to go far, go with the team". Teamwork makes the Dream work as they say. Collaborative partnerships allow for shared decision making, shared resources, shared tasks and shared risks.

Each member of MOV, as we affectionately call ourselves, comes to the table with a unique talent, ability or gift. Those gifts have been on display over the last 18 months as we have successfully co-hosted one national conference, facilitated many virtual webinars and radio shows and even now as we work on a major conference in Atlanta in early 2016. By sharing the load, the responsibility for the success or failure of the event does not fall on one person. It is shared responsibility, shared reward.

Treating everyone as equals when collaborating can open up communication and encourage ideas from all levels of the company or department, not just the managers or directors. A recent study conducted by Oracle quizzed over 900 marketing and IT leaders across 50 countries and over 500 organizations. According to this study, the most important benefit that comes from a collaborative workspace is the development of compelling marketing messages that lead users to buy more.

When true collaboration is allowed to exist minus the stigma created by class and titles, that's where the "magic" happens and everyone benefits. But for true collaboration to exist, you must check your ego at the door. MOV member Edward C. Williams sums it up this way: "It's not about ME-Go; it's about where WE-Go, so check your Ego!"

Building a Network is another benefit of collaboration. Most entrepreneurs out there operate with a kill-or-be-killed attitude, which only serves to isolate us from the lives we could potentially serve and the money we could make. I have found that collaboration allows me to create networks across disciplines and distances far and wide. These networks work with me to win new clients and customers as well as share my message to a larger audience.

The "Power of Collaboration" doesn't have to be limited to your field, business or industry. In a recent article on Entrepreneur.com, Jen Hansard, cofounder of Simple Green Smoothies advised businesses to "Don't limit yourself to connecting with people in your specific field". Their business has reached out to other industries and has been able to help them grow while the collaboration has been beneficial to them as well. Building relationships outside of your industry creates possibilities for growth and expansion. It also gets you in front of nontraditional circles of influence.

This collaboration with the "Men of Vision" has also allowed me to share my circle of influence with everybody else in the group and I dare say they have been able to grow their businesses as a result of each one of us sharing our own personal circles of influence in a collaborative effort to take everybody to the next level

COACHING and COUNSEL:

When you collaborate, you are able to utilize the strengths and skill sets of everyone involved. There are skills that you may be lacking that can be enhanced through a collaborative effort. Founding MOV member John McClung Jr. said in a recent broadcast we did on BLAB.im that, "Collaboration is a one of the things that benefited me. A lot of times you can be in an area or environment and you're sometimes by yourself from a networking standpoint. Here you have the people around you that can actually build you up".

In a collaborative arrangement, you get to learn from like mined individuals in your chosen field or in areas outside of your circle of influence. That access is critical to the growth and sustainability of your business, no matter what it may be. Within the "Men of Vision", we have accountability and empowerment coaches, leadership strategists, branding and apparel experts and book optimization success strategists. Each member brings a level of expertise to the table that is invaluable to the rest of the group.

We have collaborated and we've had some great successes individually as well as collectively as a result of this collaborative effort. Leveraging that expertise within the group in a collaborative manner has helped us all to become "Amazon Best Selling Authors". We have learned technology tricks that have allowed us to speak on different interview platforms both virtual and in person. We even host our own internet TV and radio broadcasts. Because of what we have learned through our collaborations, we now can coach others to effectively do the same things.

Many times as entrepreneurs, we think we have to do it all by ourselves. Because of this, we find ourselves "wearing too many hats". We try to do EVERYTHING instead of just focusing on SOMETHING and ultimately end up doing NOTHING! When we enter into collaborative arrangements, we are able to "take off a hat" and trust someone who has that skill set to do what we can't do. You can then get coaching from that person on the skills that can actually make you better. We see that is what is happening in this group on a daily basis. There is nothing better than to have the ability to have four other brothers around you that are experts in different fields, especially those areas in which you need help in.

In our weekly MOV meetings, we are able to bounce ideas off of each other and receive effective counsel in the process. We are able to create new strategies to help turn those ideas into viable outcomes. We are able to talk about possible pitfalls or obstacles and create contingencies to overcome them.

To be able to gain knowledge and hear other people viewpoints on a given area is priceless. It can literally mean the difference between success and failure in your business.

MOV emphasizes working together, not in a spirit of competition but through a spirit of collaboration. The person asking for the collaboration is not perceived as being weak. That person is embraced for being strong enough to tell somebody else that they were weak. That person can then collaborate with us and help us be stronger in the areas in which we were weak. It's just been one collaborative effort after the other since the first Sunday night in November 2014 all the way up to now.

I think the most powerful thing that I've learned from collaboration is counsel. Imagine that you have a whole box of puzzle pieces on the table. One thing I know is if you don't have a vision of what the final puzzle looks like, you don't have the direction you need to go to create it. That's where collaboration comes in.

When you can talk to someone who has made the puzzle before, they can show you how this piece fits and where this piece goes. Sooner or later, you have this wonderful finished product called a masterpiece. So it's that having the counsel of an apparel specialist in "I am a Testimony Clothing" that helps you take your vision and put it on your wrist or put it on your chest or put it on your head.

It's wise counsel to have someone who not only talks about rising up as a man, but shows each and every day how to rise up as a man. Counsel is someone telling you that "even coaches need coaches". It helps to be able to talk to another coach about your coaching practice or how you can be better with whatever it is you are doing.

ACCOUNTABILITY:

I am an "ACCOUNTABILITY Coach" and I tell my clients this one thing at the beginning of every coaching partnership. "A Vision with No Action will remain a Dream!" Referencing the 'do it all by myself' statement from earlier in this piece, the fear of being accountable to realizing our vision often keeps us stuck in our dreams. We don't act on our dreams and they end up going to the grave with us when we die.

Collaborations allow you the opportunity to be accountable to yourself AND someone else. It provides that extra motivation necessary to work on goals and achieve results. You know you're accountable to more than just yourself.

Accountability in collaborations are key because you can have some wonderful skill sets but you need that push from individuals who understand exactly how you fit into the group.

In some cases, accountability partners make you better because you are held accountable to be the best that you can be. They make me feel that I can actually be greater than I thought.

I recently had the opportunity to collaborate with one of my coaching clients on a book. He is a father who is raising a son with special needs. His life depends highly on different collaborations throughout the day. From the moment he wakes up, it is collaboration between the father and his wife to get his son bathed, dressed and ready for school. He collaborates with the school crossing guards to assist him in getting his son to and from the school. After school, the father collaborates with swim coaches and drum teachers to provide needed therapy and stimulation for his child.

His life is a series of collaborations with school staff, therapists, doctors, coaches and advocates to ensure his son gets the best care possible. He is accountable to his son and for his son's well being. He pushes himself to get results for his son because he knows it's his purpose. He is his dad and he is accountable.

Out of this journey with his son, this client has decided he wants to help other father's cope with raising children who have special needs. He wants to tell his story of how he has been able to do it, but he didn't know where to start. That led to a new collaboration where he leveraged my talents as a coach to walk him through the process of creating a manuscript. Then we leveraged the talents of our Book Optimization Success Strategist (B.O.S.S.), Johnny Mack and our talented graphic design specialist, Tara Gazzoulo, to create a cover design and finished book called "Thoroughly Immersed" which is due to be released in April 2016.

Out of the Dream of seeing his son be all he could be despite his challenges came this father's Vision for helping other fathers. Because he was Accountable to his son and these future fathers that he would help, he took Action and Collaborated with people who could help his Dream come true. Now his Vision is a reality. That's the Power of Collaboration.

Like my client, you probably have had many opportunities to collaborate with other people in your life and business. Have you utilized those opportunities? Have you considered the BENEFITS of collaboration? Could your business benefit from the COACHING/COUNSELING sessions that come with collaborations? Do you need ACCOUNTABILITY to someone else as to push your business to the Next Level?

It's nothing like having other people where you can extend your reach and can actually talk to people that are not necessarily your circle and vice versa. Collaboration has definitely met and exceeded my expectations from a business standpoint. From networking to directly forming new friendships, collaborative partnerships have enhanced my business and I'm sure it will do the same for you. When you can actually do things together that change people's lives, it's also a great benefit.

As an entrepreneur just getting started, you want your vision to turn it into a business. If you want to go from a small business to big business, you got to stop thinking you have to do it all by yourself. Really open yourself up to the possibility of collaboration.

I won't speak for anyone else, but again I went from not even dreaming about being an author to being a best-selling author of two books. I went from just having a few coaching clients to now consistently coaching clients. I went from speaking on my phone or on virtual platforms to speaking on stages across the country all at some point out of this collaboration.

A quote by Amy Koehler says it best. "As you navigate through the rest of your life be open to collaboration. Other people's ideals and other people are often smarter and better than you. Find a group of people who challenge and inspire you. Spend a lot of time with them and it will change your life!"

So that's what I would say to anybody who was just thinking about or has already started a business. Find yourself someone to collaborate with. If you want to get unstuck and be unstoppable, then you need some collaboration in your life.

Contact Info on Terrance Leftridge

Terrance Leftridge is best known as the Unstoppable Coach. His clients rely on his skill and expertise as an accountability Coach. Coach "T" as he is affectionately called. Is what's known as a complete coach. He is able to hone in on problem areas of your business or business plan and offer correct and considered application to put you on the path to prosperity, profits and prominence. He is the author of three Bestselling books, the third an interesting compilation that was derived from a coaching client that truly had something to say but did not know how. Terrance hosts a weekly radio program called The next level living show and can be reached at...

tleftridge@unstoppablecoaching.com

nextlevellivingshow@gmail.com

Chapter 7: Collaboration from a Pastor's Perspective

By: Pastor Jonathan Haywood

2 Timothy 1:1-10 (Scriptural Reference)

True factors of collaboration from my point of view can be a bit raw, natural, unprotected and naked. In most cases the natural state of things that we as humans might encounter when we first come in contact of a person, place or thing, we're often looking from the wrong perspective. The power of the flesh has a great impact on the human race more than any other living organism in this world! Raw thinking however comes from within and we as the creation must come to the realization it's not treated, prepared, organized nor is it polished from the authority of men. Collaboration is in fact a part of the creator's plan which we're created for. It has been His handy work and was for His pleasure, so what does that mean; HIS PLEASURE? It's quite simple to them that see through the eyes of FAITH but it's very difficult to see through the eyes FLESH!

1 Peter 2:1-15 Scriptural Reference)

True collaboration has to be real, authentic with no substitution nor artificial teamwork. Unfortunately there's a great influence of false relationship and partnership sweeping across the nation with the intent to annihilate our true function as gifted individuals. However we must come to grips with ourselves in knowing that we're all one enormous puzzle waiting to be connected. Each of us has a responsibility to understand that process validates the purpose of this mass puzzle.

Can you say UNORTHODOX? Why you ask? I'm glad you did, now let me explain. It seems as thou the world is full of individuals that are ashamed of who and what they are and everyone wants to be the person next to them. Many say I can hear that voice screaming at me saying let me out! Set me free! Who are you? Or I can't take this anymore and most of us know what we should be doing but have refused to because of the company you'll need to keep in order to be free and be your true self.

Prominent, well-known and perceptibly gifted people will forever stick out and can only hide for a little while because their gifts can't help but scream to the public, you can't keep me a secret forever!!! For this reason unorthodox gifted individuals are not chosen to remain hidden because of their abilities through unconventional, untraditional and unusual methods. Yes it's time for you to come out of your shell and be who you were designed to be because you're the puzzle piece we've been looking for.

Process Validates the Purpose

To build open collaborative communication, formation and creation of ideas, social involvement, and enthusiasm, to redevelop, regenerate, and reinstitute, spiritual growth and faith towards building a foundation of support within our communities, our cities and states.

COLLABORATED GOALS ARE THE OBJECTIVES

1. Make it known that collaboration can be a desired unity with true purpose!

2. Acknowledge the differences between collaborated basic beliefs and false philosophy!

3. Recognize the impact of collaborated history and adversity based within team members beliefs!

4. Accept that there are many paths to complete a collaborated Journey!

5. Create an opportunity to generate the opportunities to collaborate forward to the benefit for all!

THESE GOALS JOIN US TOGETHER WITH FLEXIBILITY TO ACCOMPLISH AND BUILD A TEAM!

T= Together

E= Everyone

A= Accomplishes

M= More

Leadership can influence and affect any association or company. This is based on how well they've taken the time to learn from past, present and potentially its future prospects and or opportunities, that's more than likely to be added, chosen and or to be successful. Careful and extensive consideration must be a part of what, where, when, how and why it's leadership has come to any and all of their decisions in forming an exceptionally well put together diverse collaborated people who can work as one single unit and complete any assignment.

Being fruitful has its benefits, while the results from most calculations are impressive to the naked eyes, however when the harvest doesn't reflect what's been planted the question is, didn't I plant an Orange tree? If so why are there Lemons at the base of my tree? Something's not right; could it be that you weren't paying attention when making your selections?

My point being, many Leaders have been making the same bad choices time after time because they keep choosing the same type of individuals. For this reason leaders will continue to redo, restart, reject and regret their final results. It's funny how we think we're going somewhere quick, fast and in a hurry but the fact of the mater we're still not willing to come out of the same thinking to make collective and collaborated change.

Effective workmanship speaks with a clear, precise and specific language to determine and clarify the vision calculated. A true enemy to self wouldn't just out-right kill you before he/she has had the opportunity to destroy and corrupt your integrity and influence. By doing so he/she is given an opportunity to not only destroy your image and influence but be able to turn all eyes in your direction to destroy your confidence and self-assurance.

Effective leadership must know and understand that the purpose of leading is more than putting oneself out front as the shot caller but also the protector, shield and defense. This cannot be done by one's self, but as an effort of a group of strong fearless and powerful individuals with the intent to gain the same interests, to accomplish the same goals.

Discovering your destiny should be your ultimate goal. However, when you're around others that can see your failures clearer than you and they are willing to sacrifice their own success as a person just to complete the mission. This speaks volumes concerning their character!

True leadership understands the purpose, plan and strategy for relationship through collaborating with others. They won't think nor respond to any situation due to how every person learns how and why we gather, disseminate and distribute important information. As a pastor I've had the privilege and honor to sit in many services and watch how people mimic leadership and its many forms of prejudiced behaviors! You would think that many of our spiritual leaders have learned by now that people are born to follow and they will shadow every movement as if their lives depended on it!

The behavior of false leadership in the Pulpit has corrupted and dishonored us exponentially beyond the four walls of the church into our environment and has weakened the inspiration and intimate relationship between the creator and its creation! So the question is, how do we restore this breach? We must return to the origin of why a collaborated and diverse selection of 12 men from different walks of life were called and given a vision to become fishermen of men.

Due to contrary belief, the selection of the 12 disciples wasn't based on trust but only on the fact that the creator wanted to show that the power of collaboration of individuals from different walks of life could be joined together and by the authority of the Father given the power of the Holy Ghost   and turn the world upside down in such a way that many feared just to hear them speak!

Dependable leadership suffers when the liberty of true gospel is widely rejected for the sake of fleshly desires. If the scriptures are correct, Satan has designed a plan that would disconnect, separate and isolate gifted, talented and anointed believers to feel as though there's no hope and all is lost.

Hebrews 11:1-19 (Scriptural Reference)

Antagonism within any brotherhood acts as a host with many parasites. My belief is to kill the Host and you destroy the parasites but unfortunately we are too nice and like Moses we want more mercy than discipline. The biggest challenge is for any people to live together, work together, play together and stay together. Courage as we used to know it is somewhat a thing of the past. For the most part it's like courage has changed into a challenge. If true courage is shown, it's often   criticized, intimidated and threatens to never show itself in the public's eye ever again!

A true partnership can lead to Exhaustion and cause many conflicts which turn into one big arena of criticism. Good leadership can use unwanted circumstances and situations and turn them into a collaborated opportunity to teach, instruct and or educate. So the revitalization if done correctly will restore and reactivate a healthy and energetic effort to refocus on the mission.

One thing's for sure if you've ever been to the circus they always have a Tight Rope act. They astonish everyone because of how high in the air it is and it always leaves me in amazement. How well they stay so focused, balanced and disciplined, now imagine if our relationship had to depend on how well we could follow those three simple but complex correlations.

Now take a look out over the audience and see how many would respond to how well we can use the power of collaboration to motivate, stimulate and inspire. Throughout my life I've been given a multitude of challenges, but somehow I always believed there's a better life to live. It will take the right connection of individuals in my life to make it happen.

Learning to lean into the direction of the storm taught me that I could still travel no matter how fast the wind might blow. It's also unquestionable not to believe that someone has given you a hundred dollars bill when the person is standing in front of you and someone standing next to you was used as a witness. What I'm simply saying is, if you were to take time to look back over your life you'd surely see that we've been given gifts and talents. You were not made by your own hands but by something more foolproof, unmanned and an unlimited amount of rescores that will never run out. Never give up and never stop pushing into your place of power, position and possession.

Our service to one to another is our most prized possession. For it is within us to serve, give and present. What would the world be like if we didn't serve one another, love one another share with one another in the many forms of service we can.

Strength is truly an understatement. If by chance you've ever had a broken foot, back and even your little pinky finger, it would take more than a couple of pills to help you handle the pain and God forbid the time it takes for healing and a full recovery. In all sincerity we all possess an inner strength that's consistently under attack but is at the same time ready to give you aid in the most unusual way. It produces a comfort just by making contact with others who believe just as you believe and that's why It's said in (Amos 3:3 Can two walk together, except they be agreed?)..

Our power as one depends upon our willingness to collaborate as one and to protect our weak. As if to say *one for all and all for one*. It would be mere ambition and pride that arises within us to attack our sinful nature and these are definitely the pros and cons of collaborating, among not only with leadership but even to the common person who are faced with difficult and stressful situations that might accrue on a day to day bases.

They say attitude determines altitude, well I believe that it's much deeper than we see from the outside looking in. Ever seen the elephants flapping their ears in the zoo? We will soon come to understand that it was only trying to keep the flies and bugs from getting inside and to close to its eardrum. I believe we too should take the same approach when someone tries to whisper something that could penetrate our connection and detour the mission.

It take more work to put something together than it takes for someone with the wrong intention to take it apart, also you've heard the expression if it's not broken don't try to fix it!

Often I've wondered, why is there more emphasis and importance placed on being accepted and or rejected by others who are no different nor any more so important then you are. I mean if I have a car and it's not as high priced as yours, what makes your car better? If I'm able to start mine every morning the same as yours and both are working what's the difference? I'm living, roof over my head, children eating every night what's the difference? My point is these thoughts weaken and sows discord within the brotherhood and it's a poison that can't be treated but must be removed out of the thought process.   If not a difference of opinion will continue to establish boundaries to destroy and eat away fellowship among the brethren.

There's one thing for sure, many will continue to try and eat away at your faith, trust and belief in life, liberty and love but at what point do you understand that it's all opinion and these are the people that are asleep to truth, passion, strength and the possibilities of your endless abilities to become whatever, wherever, whenever, whoever and however! It's time for all who have come into the knowledge of who you are to stand together, fight together and become enlightened together.

Jeremiah 1: 4-10 (Scriptural Reference)

As a young man I was never taught how to establish a good name in my community. Nor was I ever taught how to conduct myself as a man who could be trusted. However I knew at an early age that I was multitalented and very skilful as a singer, so I pursued a singing career, landed my first album at 17yrs. and my second at the age of 19yrs. With very little help I accomplished what I could with the assistance of my mother and uncle, I can see now the importance of having a well put together group of individuals from different walks of life with the same vision. They must be very innovative, tenacious with a strong desire that are well able to maintain, advocate and support the vision with potency.

Subsequently, sometimes staying with a collaborated vision means there are going to be pitfalls, difficulties and complications. Nevertheless, these are the moments you pull your team together, open up the think tank and allow their various gifts and talents do what they do best. Before you now it the problems will soon reveal the blessings behind the situation. You will see that it was nothing more than a test and trial that leaves you to believe that once again process validates purpose!!!

A room full of gifted individuals who think the same, love the same things, drive the same cars, live in the same neighborhoods, wouldn't be what you would call the ideal type of collaborators. They couldn't possibly make the right choices for our children's future, and they certainly couldn't be the next clothing designers nor should they be given the opportunity to be the next line of architects to build bridges in the future. We must become the authenticity of true reality and realize that we're different for a reason, but through our differences we've created just what was intended, the first living and moving human puzzle, so come join us because we have a perfect place that you'll fit! **The Power of Collaboration**

Info on Pastor Jonathan Haywood

Pastor Jonathan Haywood is unconventional in every since of the word. He is enjoying a successful career with NASA (No he's not a rocket scientist but he knows a few) He is the pastor of a local church and is also the host of a local television show. Jonathon is unafraid to challenge the loftiest of Religious stalwart and is yet humble enough to be a student and learn. It is with that servants heart that pastor Haywood Brings attention to the body to step up and become all you were meant to be. Jonathan loves nothing more than sharing the Good News that God loves you and would love for you to Prosper...but he ain't playing. Pastor Jonathan can be reached at...

jehaywood.haywood@gmail.com

He is available for Coaching, Keynote Speaking, Conferences, Seminars, panels, webinars and presentations

Chapter 8: A Collaborative B.A.L.L (Born Again Lord Led)

By: John McClung Jr.

L ife leaves its landmarks. In October of 1980 I set out on my own to conquer the world, but I really was just trying to leave home and venture out on my own. I wanted to make my mark on the world and although I was a young 18 year old ambitious young man, I had big hopes and aspirations as well as dreams.

I grew up in a home full of love, closeness, spirituality and discipline. You see. I grew up in the home of a Pastor and there were so many days I was reminded of that. I am not saying that growing up as a preacher's kid was bad, but it certainly was not easy. There were many days that often reminded me of the things I thought I missed and I certainly thought I was supposed to be bad because I always heard that, 'we were the worst kids in the world.'

There were times that I didn't think I could ever be a good kid, because of what I had heard and I often wondered where my friends being told the same thing. I did understand that these words were coming from other people, my parents never called us the worst kids in the world and that was some comfort, but when we stepped outside of the house it was a different world.

When I decided to leave home 3 months after I graduated I wasn't just leaving the family, or friends or the neighborhood, I was leaving behind and identity that wasn't for me. When you grow up in a prominent pastor's home, you can lose your identity, for that fact you can lose your identity in any home if you allow it to happen. Having a father who was faithful to God and his ministry placed an added amount of pressure on others to label me as 'the one' to be like my father, I was supposed to be the preacher.

Well, needless to say as a young kid I didn't know what or who I was going to be, but I knew I wanted to make an impact on the world with my God given skills, gifts and talents. The one thing I wanted most like many who read this, was to create something I could be proud of and kingdom build with it.

I often wondered how many other people had loss their dream because someone had already identified who they were going to be and never really had a chance to realize their own potential or speak to who it was they wanted to be. I knew that was not how I saw my life and it was a struggle to separate who others wanted me to be and who I was going to be. I can't say I remember my father ever saying he wanted me to be like him, but I guess he didn't need too, others were doing it for him.

It was difficult working in the shadows of a God fearing man and wanting to have a voice that screamed, 'I just want to be me!' Have you ever just wanted to scream and let the world know, 'I am not like anyone else?' And believe me, being like my father was not a bad thing, but not being me was the thing that I could not get over.

Some may have believed I was fighting the inevitable. You see, I had some of the traits of a servant's heart and the ability to teach, I got it honest, just like any other kid who watched their parents closely you just pick up some things that work for you even though they might not be you. For so many years I watched my father prepare the message that he was going to bring to his congregation on Sunday morning and it was amazing. You see each week he had a way of preparing by reading, studying, breaking things down, it was what is considered a routine to most of us, but at a young age I really didn't understand that concept, I just knew he stayed up late each night reading different books and writing notes.

But as time went on, I realized he was perfecting what he was good at and that was teaching the Word of God! As I became more aware of how engaged he was in getting better at presenting, teaching and serving others with the messages he gave, I recognized that this was his calling, it was the business he was to be about, he was being led to handle God's business!

At 18, I thought I was ready to leave the nest, the confines of a warm and loving home, a mother who thought the world of her oldest son and wanted so much to have the best for me in everything and a father who would have loved to have me follow in his footsteps. I knew that would make him proud! But, that would have made him proud, what about me?

I saw so many others who decided to listen to the people they were surrounded by and not become the person they were supposed to be. I watched many waste their talents, gifts and abilities listening to others. I couldn't see how they could let their life go to waste or be a victim of what others wanted for them when they wanted something else and was too afraid to go and get it, too afraid to step out and find their own identity, kick the box of being a duplicate instead of being the unique person God intended them to be, that was not going to happen to me.

I was fortunate to know early in life that despite what others said I would be, I knew that despite the words that were being spoken into my life, there was a different plan for me, there was different path, a different dream, a different reason to live. I knew that I had some traits that would allow me to help others in my own way, speak in to others in my own way and change lives for the better, including mine. I didn't know how long it would take, but I knew that is what I was supposed to do. I knew that there was a business that I needed to be about as well as start and I know there are many who want to have a business that is Faith based and are hesitant in following their heart and passion.

When I thought about leaving, I remembered all those days I had to go to church, it was all I knew. Some days as a little kid we were the church. I remembered all the fun I missed out on, some of the places we could not go, things I could not participate in, it seems like I had a tough childhood, in some sense yes, but in other ways no. I just wanted to have the ability of not being judged, growing up with all eyes on your every move, that is some crazy pressure for a kid! But I didn't choose the life, my parents did and these were some of the challenges that came with that decision.

The difficult part of choosing to venture out on your own, is the unknown. I really had no idea what purpose was, I did read some books, listened to some tapes, went to some seminars and motivational speeches, including the ones I heard every week from my father. I was just running from everything that was not me, I was running from what I thought was the inability to choose who I wanted to be, I was running from the safety of wisdom and experience, heck, I was just running, but you can't get away from your God given purpose.

Do you know what that is like? Can you identify with just running? Maybe from your past, or from a bad relationship, broken home, bad marriage, crazy job, and you have no idea where you are going. I know I am not by myself when I speak about this, but that is how I felt. It was a transition time that I had to face and as bad and my parents wanted me to stay, as I sat across from them and told them I wanted to leave and go my own way. I had to be about what God wanted for my life, even if I didn't know.

I used school as my shelter for leaving but I knew I wanted a taste of the world, my own experiences, my own failures, my own challenges, my own obstacles as well as my own successes. I wanted to prove that I didn't have to be like someone else to succeed, although I still wanted them to be proud of me, I had to let them see their son needed his own space. Do you need your own space? It doesn't have to be hidden in leaving home, it could be you need some breathing room, you need to follow your dreams act on your vision, pursue your own goals, whatever it is, only you know.

I wanted to create experiences and opportunities that would help me make a difference in the lives of others. There was something in me saying, you have something unique and you need to find it no matter how long it takes. Was it tough out there, heck yeah! Did I run into things I wasn't prepared for and had to figure it out, you better believe it, did life knock me down and say to me, 'what are you going to do?' Absolutely! And I know if you are reading this, it has done the same thing to you as well, it's just the way life is. But when God is on your side, you can do anything you set your heart and mind too.

I remember telling myself, 'all that you do is not just for you and it is not for everybody, but if you can help somebody, then it will eventually affect everybody' and so my goal was to take this journey as a young man and grow into a man that could make an impact on others by sharing the experiences that help me grow into someone that they could identify with. Did life take some things from me? Yes it did! You see, leaving home and making it this far didn't keep me from getting scars, it didn't keep me from losing jobs, it didn't keep from losing a home or being homeless, it didn't keep me from not having any money and knowing where my next meal was coming from, it didn't have mercy on me when I was crying out for help, No! Life just kept on teaching me lessons, the kind of lessons that helped me learn to see that I needed to have a plan, I needed to have some type of strategy that would get me through. And the tough part was, where do I start? I wanted to build something that would last!

And I just bet that that life has given you some type of fight, it has you in the ring and you are taking some punches that you did not see coming, you have had some blows that caught you off guard and you may even have had to take a standing eight count because those punches left you in a daze! Well, I understand and you don't have to be one who can't fight back, or not have a game plan to get through the rounds. You can go back to your corner, pull yourself together, listen to your trainer and come back out swinging like I did. Because, you have to complete the assignment given to you by God and that is not going to be easy at all, but you have everything in you to make it happen.

Yeah, that 18 year old teenager had to go through some difficult rounds, he had to take some significant blows, even having to deal with the loss of the most influential man in his life. You see growing up is not easy to do, because some may think it's based on age, No! Experience has taught me it is those very things that you endure that provide the lessons you can help someone else with. You see unless you have been in a fight, you can't become a champion and the only the only way you can share your Testimony is if you have gone through a test. And, that is what gave me the business I have today!!

If you see yourself in these words, if you have identified with not having a voice of your own, if you have been one who has been beat up by life, keep reading! I am going to share some things that helped me get to where I am today. I want to share some principles that have been a part of me learning how to live my dream, how to shape my life and how to impact the lives I have had the opportunity of crossing during this journey and how to take the vision given to me and create a business that will change and affect lives. I had no idea the road I would be taken down, but today I understand why I was supposed to leave the comforts of home and journey down this path towards my destiny.

I wandered what it would be like when I had a chance for my voice to be heard, to share my experiences, my wisdom and pour into the life of others. I no longer have to wonder because

I am doing just that! And as you continue to read, I want to share just a few principles that guided my life and helped me to see the dreams I thought that were never possible become a reality. You see if you are anything like me, and you are a dreamer, you need to know that Dreams can come true

A New Vision for Victory

Before leaving home, my father gave me some advice and he would always give me one word whenever I called him. It didn't have to be a long drawn out conversation, he wasn't going to do that, he was just going to lay on my heart and mind a word that would take me through the next few weeks. So, I am going to share a few things from the word he gave me and then I am going to share some principles that helped me get through some difficult challenges, tough times and create a mindset, that there was nothing I could not accomplish.

I know you are wondering, what is the word he is going to share that can help me in my life? Well the word is VISION, A word I am sure you have heard before. The next few minutes of reading I want to provide some definition to this word that shaped my life and helped me go through every Test and become a Testimony.

You see, the word Vision means: The manner in which one sees or conceives of something. Have you when reading this definition felt any of these things? I know I did and I begin to dig a little deeper and find out why my dad chose this word that would change my life in so many ways. Here is what I learned, that Vision is what gets you up off the couch, it is what makes you dream, it is what keeps you going.

One of my favorite book, well really my favorite book, says 'Delight thyself in the Lord and he shall give thee the Desires of thine heart'. Now Delight means to pamper - so you have to learn how to pamper your Dreams, Purpose and Visions.

I had heard this on so many occasion and I am sure you probably have as well, but I want to shed a totally different light on this as you read further. What Vision do you have for yourself? What Vision have you not accomplished? What Vision if accomplished would totally change your life?

I worked for an Airlines and I had the opportunity to work out on the runway and I had the chance to learn some lessons on the runway that were applicable to life and the Visions we have for our life. I watched so many people live their travel dreams when they got on those planes. But, here is something you may have never known, the instrument used to move the plane from the gate on to the runway. This instrument needed to be attached to the plane in order for the plane to be given the all go sign and pushed back from the gate and on to the runway so it can prepare to take off- That tool used was called a TUG.

One of the life lessons learned on that runway was that everyone with vision for their life, first has to have a Tug. I understood that there has to be a tug of some sort for you to go after the visions of your heart. So, what is tugging at you to do what it is you want to do? Is that new job tugging at you, what about writing that new book or becoming a teacher, is it that new relationship you want to start or getting on stage to sing that new song? Understand and know, there is a Tug on your life that wants you to have the Visions of your heart.

When have a Vision for your life, you must understand the first thing:

You must be Vision Specific – What do I mean by that? Glad you asked. When you begin to go after your goals, your dreams, your vision, when you know and understand that there is a tug on you to do something, you must be very specific about it. You need to be very clear before you begin to chase after it. This is a principle I didn't really get until later, but I want you to get it now, 'That which you are specific about, will come about.' You must and again, I say must have clarity about what it is you want for your life. You cannot just make a decision and not have full understanding of why you are doing it. Your specific decision must change a life, help a life and add value to a life.

You must also understand that you are the Vessel for your vision. No one else is responsible for what has been given to you by God but you. Just as Noah was responsible for being the Vessel for the Ark, you are going to be the only one that accomplishes the vision given to you regardless of what others may say or do, or even If someone has a similar idea. They won't be able to make your vision happen the way you will, because it is only meant for you!

Second, before an individual decides to go to the airport and get on a flight, there is some strategy involved. You don't just pick any place to go, you have a vision to go somewhere specific, right and then you create a strategy to get there, this is called being Vision Strategic. There is strategy to the Vision you have for yourself. There are steps you need to take to be successful. Before you decided to move forward on your purpose or journey, you need to make sure you have a plan. Now, when I left home I didn't quite have a plan and some of my failures proved it. But from those non planned lessons, I quickly learned that if I was going to be able to have my tug get me on to the runway, I needed to make sure I had a good flight plan. That plan can evolve over time, but be sure that you have one.

There will also be an investment you must make for your vision and dreams to come true. There are many ways that you will have to invest in what you are trying to accomplish. Your time, effort, willingness to put in long hours, money, travel, headaches – Yes! There are going to be some investments such as seminars, books, tapes, conferences, coaching and training. For you to see your vision come true, you have to be willing to make some investment.

The third thing I want to share about Vision, is that you must be strong about the choices you make for your life, in other words you must be Vision strong. You need to have such conviction about what you want to do in life, that you eat, sleep, drink and breathe it every day. Being Vision strong means, that everything about you will stand strong for what you believe for yourself, that you cannot be moved, your Vision is so strong that it can stand any test. Do you have a vision for your life that strong? Do you see yourself doing what you want to do no matter what is being said to you? Do you really believe you can make your dreams come true? I hope so.

I didn't know that when I left my parent's home, that I was Vision strong. I wanted so badly to make it on my own and succeed. I know that there is something in you that you feel so strongly about that you would be willing to leave things behind and go after it, what is that Vision?

That is part of the Sacrifices that you are going to have to make to see your vision come to life. There is no victory for your vision without sacrifice. There will be many people in your life left behind because of the sacrifices you make for your vision, relationships that may be placed on the back burner, life adjustments that you may not have been ready for. To complete what has been given to you, you will make some sacrifices that just may change your life.

The fourth thing I want to share, is that you must be Vision Driven. Wow, what do I mean by that it almost sounds like being Vision strong but there is a difference? What I learned about this principle, about being driven, that even in moments of weakness, there is nothing that will stop you from going after your dream. Having the drive to move forward despite the haters in your life, to have the drive despite those who want to sabotage your dreams, the drive to continue even when you don't see a light at the end of the tunnel.

That Drive, you see, that Drive will move you from the gate despite the weather conditions, that drive will keep you moving toward your destiny even when you seem like you are in a holding pattern, that drive will make you believe that all things are possible even when others say it is not, that drive will take you from the curb, to the gate, down the tunnel, onto the plane, out to the runway and into the air – That is the drive you want to have for your life, you must be Vision Driven!

Be willing to Inspire people with your vision. You see, your vision must inspire others to go after what their want for their lives, if your vision does not inspire people, you might want to check and see if it is on track for what you should be doing. As I spoke of Noah, the vision to build the Ark was inspiring, it was the longest vision endured, he saved lives by completing his vision and he is the only man known to build an Ark that we still talk about today. That is Inspiring!

There are also many opportunities for your vision that you cannot pass up and over look. You must be aware of those who bring them into your path. Sometimes you can be so focused on making your vision happen, that you miss the opportunities that are around you that can help you accomplish the task in a simpler way. Yes, opportunities abound, but you must be willing to see them for what they are so that as they come, you can become victorious as your vision change lives.

Lastly, but not least, one of the lesson that was most important and I hope you see why this played a significant role for me and I hope for you as well. You must be Vision connected. Well john, what do you mean by that? Glad you asked. This is where my foundation comes from, this is what got me through so many storms this is what I believe for you will take you to the other side!

To be vision connected, means to be connected to your source no matter what you are going through. Growing up in Church, I knew and understood what my source was and how much I heavily had to lean on it. Now, God is the source of my life and there is no shame in me saying that. You may see something as a different source that sustains you and keeps you going and that is fine, but know and understand you must stay connected to that source as you are being pushed toward your purpose and dreams.

There was also a lesson I learned about vision that really falls in line with these principles. You see, when you know that you are the vessel for your vision, you also must know that your Vision is also necessary and needed. Noah's Ark, was necessary as his vision and it was needed to complete it, Moses was necessary for leading the people out of bondage and he was needed for the task and assignment – You are necessary for your vision and you are needed so it can change the world.

I know my faith in God kept me going when I had nothing else and in order to have the Visions of your heart, remember you must delight yourself in your source – in other words stay constantly connected to it, be grateful for it be thankful that it is part of your life and journey. Being connected daily, helped me get through some really tough times. It helped me know that I was the vessel for what God had for me and I was needed. I know that I had the prayers of my parents over me as I walked out that door to take on the world and every day since, I know that it is for that reason I am here today sharing this story, principles and journey with you.

I hope that the journey that was shared by me will in some way shed a little light, give some guidance awaken some Vision in your heart to move you through the terminal, to the gate, down the tunnel, onto the runway so that you can take flight! You can be victorious, why because through it all while you are in the clouds enjoying this part of your journey, you can look at all the trials, challenges, obstacles and test and know that You Are A Testimony!

Info on John McClung Jr.

John McClung Jr. is a pastors son and an entrepreneur at heart. He is the founder and sole proprietor of "I Am A Testimony" Clothing line. He is the Author of Amazon Best Selling Books, all accomplished in the year 2015. He is able to create unique and wearable branding of trademarks and slogans. Mr. McClung is a studious Speaker and is proud to be a Ruben West Certified Black Belt Speaker. "Motivational Speakers". In addition he is a Radio and Television artist with a love and affection to see people motivated to their greatness. His words and actions help deliver that promise. John offers a precise coaching concept that zeros in on what a person needs not necessarily what they want. He can be reached at...

iamatestinomy@yahoo.com

He is available for Coaching, Keynote Speaking, Conferences, Seminars, panels, webinars and presentations

Afterword

By Dr. Ruben West

I have the great distinction of working with gifted men and women from across the country in my speaker training camps and workshops. When the Men of Vision asked that I share in this collaborative anthology, I leaped at the chance. My philosophy has always been, " help enough others win and you win as well".

It is not often that I am overwhelmed. Well let me say I am Overwhelmed at the prospect of what these authors have offered. Each one has presented a succinct expression of what Collaboration can and should mean to others. As I poured over each chapter I was enlightened and encouraged, dare I say empowered. The unique and specific focus that was applied to a singular subject from 8 different perspectives was amazing and assuring. It is indeed refreshing to know that all of our own experiences and examples prepare us for a unique field of battle.

This Field is all too often replete with warriors seeking to compete with one another. How delightfully reassuring it is that men can be on that field and co-operate and collaborate for the greater good of the whole, which lends itself to individual accomplishment. As I train speakers and coaches to enter the arena of motivation and inspiration I equip them with the power of Collaboration. They must know that alone they can only go so far, with the collaborative efforts of others they can conquer the mountain in front of them and be aided to climb others as well.

The Power of Collaboration will lift you out of the doldrums and place you into a better place of winning and working toward your goal of going to your next level. As I read each chapter, I found myself thinking about my own vision and how I was able to reach more of my goals due to the collaborative interaction with others.

I shudder to think where I would be had it not been for the synergistic benefits derived from not only working with others but ultimately working for others and they in turn worked for me. This is a much better model than selfishness and competition. This book is going to help a lot of people scale up to Live their Best Life

Dr. Ruben West

Live Your Best Life

Dr. Ruben West is a Multiple Best Selling Author, Speaker and Les Brown trained Platinum Speaker. He is an accomplished entrepreneur and the founder of the Black Belt Speakers. He has appeared on radio and Network television. Dr. West has spoken on stage with many of today's top Motivational leaders including Les Brown, The Get motivated tour, Dr Willey Jolley and others . He has been featured on international digital platforms and speaks to youth groups across the country.

Dr. Ruben West is a Keynote platform speaker and is available at info@rubenwest360.com

RubenWest360.com